ANN JAMIESON

FOR THE

LOVE

OF THE

HORSE

VOLUME II

Note for Librarians: A cataloguing record for this book is available from Library and Archives Canada at www.collectionscanada.ca/amicus/index-e.html

CONTENTS

FAMILY

TEACHERS

HUMANS HELPING HORSES

HORSES HELPING HUMANS (AND HORSES)

OVERSEAS

LOVE AT FIRST SIGHT

BEATING THE ODDS

WHOOPS!

HORSE CRAZY....

AND MORE...

INTRODUCTION

Anyone who loves horses will appreciate this book. These are all true stories: stories about the bond between horses and humans. That bond is not particular to one breed or one discipline; it encompasses everyone who spends time in any way with these incredibly generous souls.

I wrote this book to celebrate that bond, to honor the horse. Horses bring so many gifts into our lives in so many ways.

This book is a thank you—to my horses, to horses everywhere.

Cover photo Todd Karn on Annie's Homer
Tobé Saskor Photography

Back Cover photo Gillette at Gillette's Castle in
East Haddam, Connecticut
Terry Joseph photo

Acknowledgements

Thank you to everyone who shared their stories with me and to all the horses who have changed our lives. Thanks to the town of Kent where I live, for the whole community's tremendous support for my book, to all the stores in town who carried it: the House of Books, Country Clothes, Kent Video (sadly no longer in business), Kent Green Hair Salon, the Fife and Drum Gift Shop, Country Feed and the Kent Gulf station. Thanks to Carol Hall in the IGA for your constant support and interest, to Karen Chase for your support and for getting the word out in the newspaper.

Thanks to Natalia Zunino, for once again stepping in to edit when I got stuck and to June Zettelmeyer for your willingness to always take a look at another story. To Beth Vaculik, for your enthusiasm, your patience in unlocking software/computer secrets and your vision for producing a more beautiful book. Thanks to Hobbes who sat right next to my laptop, stepping on a particular key if it seemed appropriate. Thank you to all of the Mancuso family for spreading the word about it wherever you go. Thanks to Tommy Passalaqua, John Soto and Jeff Johnston for their untiring efforts to help me with stories and marketing, to Chris and Lori Barnard for your support and to all of the tack stores, feed stores and gift shops who welcomed the book with open arms. And thank you to everyone who's ever stopped me at a book signing or horse show to tell me how much you enjoyed my book. Your kind words are so appreciated!

THIS BOOK IS DEDICATED IN MEMORY OF
ANNIE'S HOMER
AND
TOP GUN'S FLY FREE

FAMILY

⟿ TWISTER

His name had been chosen three years before he was born. His mom was her first reining horse, Double R Odds, a horse she won a class on at the intensely competitive Quarter Horse Congress. A year later she placed second in a huge class there on his dad, Reebok's Kid.

As a trainer Heather Servies Johnson never got to spend much time with a horse. She would work with them for a few months, and back to their owner they would go.

That all changed with the birth of Doubleknotyoureeboks. Born in 2002, he was the first baby she bred with the intent to raise and train herself. This was, and would remain her horse, a horse she had a chance to develop a tremendous relationship with.

Heather was in for a bit of a surprise when he was born. He was ugly. Quite ugly. He had a big forehead that was in no way cute and cuddly like most foals. The mark on that big forehead resembled a tornado, and resulted in his barn name of Twister.

Luckily, in time he did become cute. His unusual coloring, a sorrel with flaxen mane and tail with blonde highlights, was pretty. And Heather loved working with him. He was such a good baby, so patient, so easy.

However, he was quite vocal. Sensing his royal heritage and future greatness, he announced it to the world at every opportunity.

Twister had an interesting childhood. Heather "dragged him everywhere" she went. Just because she had a baby now didn't mean she could ignore her duties as a trainer. If she had to go somewhere else—a show, another barn—no problem, she'd just pop him in the trailer and off they went.

At two, the easy baby went through a transformation. He hit the terrible twos, hit it in spades. The suggestions to Heather were unanimous. Geld him!

Luckily Heather ignored them. She trusted her instincts: this horse was special. She would ride out the terrible twos and keep her horse whole.

A year later Doubleknotyourreeboks proved her faith in him more than justified. She and Twister qualified for the finals for the Reining Futurity at the Quarter Horse Congress in Columbus, Ohio. After the first go-round, Heather sat in the stands with her then fiancé Kyle Johnson, waiting to find out the results. She was so nervous that she was afraid she might throw up.

She needn't have worried. She was competing the best horse she's ever trained or sat on. For Twister, it all comes naturally. All Heather has to do is "let him do it for me." Still, she laughed when she got her draw. It was between two of the biggest names in reining history, Tim McQuay and Shawn Flarida.

Not only did three year old Twister and Heather qualify for the final go-round, they won their class, the Intermediate Open Reining Futurity. It was the biggest class she had ever won, and the first class she'd won since her victory with his Mom. And it was a huge victory, a victory over many of the legends of the reining world.

Winning the class, they tied with Bill Horn, another legend and one of the founders of the National Reining Horse Association. Meeting him, to Heather was "like meeting a rock star." And she was particularly impressed when Tim and Shawn came up and congratulated her.

When Heather had looked around at the famous horses and riders she was competing against, she'd been intimidated. But Twister was having none of it. He had told the world that he was special and he had come here to prove it. Heather was amazed, that, although he was such a young horse, Twister just carried her right through. Right through to a victory.

That victory not only meant a lot to her, but it proved just how much she could trust her horse. Twister is always a superb competitor who never misbehaves. He has "taught me as much as I've taught him." In addition, he's made it so much fun. "This," says Heather "is what it is supposed to feel like."

Although Heather has received a lot of big offers for Twister, she knows she couldn't sell him. "He's come to mean a lot to me." Besides, "I see such a big future for him!"

The easy baby has resurfaced in a top notch show horse and well behaved stud. Kids at Heather's barn have no problem working with Twister. They lead him, groom him, and took it upon themselves this year to work Twister through his intense fear of water.

The big brave stallion who wasn't afraid of anything wouldn't go within ten feet of water. Many of the horses at Heather's Creekside Reining in Georgia enjoy a wade or a swim after work. Not Twister. Not until the kids got hold of him. Each day Twister would get closer to the water, until the day he placed one foot in it. Cheers erupted all around!

When Twister finally submitted and walked in and waded across, it was a huge event and a party was given in his honor. Now he loves the water. And the kids are proud of their accomplishment.

Twister's first crop of babies will soon be on the ground. Heather rode his mother and father, and has developed with him everything that a relationship between horse and human can be. Watching his babies romp around the farm will be "pure joy" says Heather. The waiting is killing her! The legacy that started years before his birth, continues.

⟶ FROLIC

For forty five years Janice Callahan has owned and worked with horses. She teaches riding for a living. She's seen a lot of horses. But none like Frolic.

Janice started riding when she was nine, taking lessons at a barn called Wilmont Riding Club in Eastchester, New York. Flame, her first horse, was a school horse she purchased when she was 14. Flame was 14 as well.

By the time they were both in their mid-20's, Flame had developed severe arthritis in his knee. He couldn't continue to work, so Janice started to look for another horse.

She looked at a friend's farm, located in Bethlehem, Connecticut. There she found a pretty bay Thoroughbred filly with a star on her forehead. Frolic 'N Me, at just two, wasn't broke yet, but she was sweet and had the "kind eye" prized by horsepeople around the world. She was also very reasonably priced, a big consideration as Janice had only recently gotten married.

Janice was thrilled when she brought her new filly home. She couldn't wait to ride her! But she knew better than to rush things. She spent months lunging and longlining her pretty filly, teaching her the groundwork so important for her future training. She was impressed. Not only was the filly beautiful and sweet, she was athletic and level headed as well. She was eager to work, and enjoyed the process of learning.

Finally, the big day came. Janice was able to ride her young horse. Frolic didn't bat an eye. She didn't buck; she didn't protest in any way. She just accepted it as part of her job.

The more Janice got to know Frolic, the better she liked her. As a three year old, Frolic went to her first show, where Janice took her in a young hunter division. They were champion. And that was only the beginning.

No matter what Janice asked, Frolic said yes. The bright bay filly just couldn't do enough to please. In hunter classes, she tucked her knees up to her chest, showing exemplary form, and she won flat classes as well. Janice showed her in equitation, dressage, and eventing, and they even went foxhunting.

Then Janice tried hitching her up to a cart. No problem: Frolic took to that just as well as everything else.

When Janice first purchased Frolic, she boarded her at a nearby barn. Then she and her husband bought their own place, and Frolic moved in with them. The small farm did not have a tractor. It needed one. The ring needed to be dragged, the fields needed to be dragged. Janice came up with a solution. She put a heavy duty breast collar on Frolic, hitched her to the old drag, and then sat on her with a halter and two leadlines. The young Thoroughbred, bred and raised to run races, never complained. Show horse? Pleasure horse? Work horse? It didn't matter to her: "just show me what you want and watch me do it" was her attitude.

Janice's two daughters, Kara and Heather also rode Frolic. As young children Frolic had pulled them around on a sled while Janice sat on her back. Janice never doubted her mare, she knew she was perfect with the kids, that they were always safe with Frolic. She continued to prove she could do it all.

At a show at Wildaire Farm Kara showed Frolic in the walk-trot division while Heather rode in the walk/trot/canter division. Kara wasn't all that interested in riding, but Heather continued. Soon Heather was doing crossrails, then children's hunters. She would show Frolic one day and Janice would show the mare the next day in First Level Dressage. Frolic would put them both in the ribbons.

Janice bred Frolic three times, but she never managed to duplicate the mare. She still has one of Frolic's sons, but he wasn't like his mother. She was one of a kind. We all treasure our "once in a lifetime horse" and hold them in our hearts forever. For Janice Callahan, that was Frolic.

⟿ Got Milk "Rock Star"

He thinks he's a rock star. And why not? He's got the looks. A velvety black coat accented with sparkling white socks and an attitude that says, "Hey, you! Pay attention! A star has arrived."

And the girls? He kisses the girls all the time. He rolls his lips up and plants a wet one smack on their face. In fact, he goes a little bit over the line, just like any rock star. He grabs the zippers on their coats and pulls them open.

Got Milk is a pony who has no clue about his species. Equine? What's that? I'm human and I don't know what your problem is. I don't even associate with those four legged creatures: my family and friends have two legs only.

He does know how to perform. When he's practicing without an audience, he might pin his ears or get a tad lazy. But in the ring? People watching? Whoa, watch out, competition. The ears are pricked, and he is ON.

Judges can't help but notice, and Got Milk and his owner, Stephanie Moscove, have wiped up in the short stirrup division, winning the hunter division in the Connecticut Hunter Jumper Association, and taking third in short stirrup equitation. Moving on to Children's Pony Medal classes they placed in the top 12 in the Marshall and Sterling League finals. This pony is all show biz.

He's got a sense of humor too. Be careful what you put down anywhere within his reach. Fellow boarder Lauren Fisher at Michele Goodrich's Well-a-Way Farm happened to put her grooming box within reach of Got Milk's stall. She walked away to get something, leaving it unattended. When she returned, it was nowhere to be seen.

15

"I'm losing my mind!" thought Lauren. "I know it was there!" She walked up and down the aisle, looking for the box. "What could have happened to it?"

What could have happened was a mischievous black pony. When the box was discovered in a corner of his stall, Got Milk looked quite pleased with himself. "Well, you should have known better than to leave it there!" he seemed to imply.

Stephanie Moscove had decided to quit riding when Got Milk (Jacques) appeared in her life. The pony she had been riding always gave her a hard time. He was a bit wild and difficult. Then he dumped her and she got hurt in the process. That's enough, she said. I don't want to ride any more.

Laura, Stephanie's mother, hated to see her daughter having a hard time. The barn was supposed to be her escape, a place to have fun. She knew she had to find a nice pony to lease for her daughter.

A friend of a friend had heard about a pony up in Massachusetts, so Laura and Stephanie took a ride up to see him.

Stephanie wasn't particularly enthusiastic. She was very tentative around the pony. She didn't want to ride anymore and didn't want to be there. Besides, she was a small child and he was a large pony. He looked huge to her and that was frightening, especially after the experience she had just had. They drove home.

But the trainer offered Laura a deal she couldn't refuse. They could try the pony for a few weeks at no cost. What could they lose?

As it turned out they had everything to gain. Stephanie was young and didn't have much experience. Jacques took charge, directing their rides. "Just hold on and I'll take care of it," was his advice to Stephanie.

As time went on and Stephanie gained experience, the balance shifted. Now they were working together as a team.

Jacques will do anything Stephanie asks of him, and he is very protective of his teammate. At one show when Stephanie fell off, onlookers remarked on how careful he was not to injure her. He contorted his body so much in order not to step on her that it was obvious he would break his own leg before he would hurt her.

When Laura and Stephanie pull up to the barn, Jacques tears down the hill from his paddock to greet them. Riding Jacques is more than just about competing to Stephanie: it's about their relationship, the partnership they share.

It didn't take Laura long to realize that this pony was too precious to the family to continue working off of a lease. They had to own him. Got Milk added immeasurably to their lives. He "just makes everything a little bit brighter," says Laura.

She purchased him secretly, without telling Stephanie, planning to surprise her for Christmas. Then she bought a name plate for his stall and wrapped and stored it for Christmas.

But the plan got scrapped when Stephanie was sick and had to stay home from school for a while. She was miserable: her body hurt and she was depressed.

Laura knew she needed to cheer her daughter up. And she had just the thing.

She brought Stephanie the wrapped nameplate. "Oh, crafts," said Stephanie when she picked up the package. Laura often bought Stephanie crafts when she was ill or laid up to help her pass the time.

But when Stephanie opened the package she discovered it wasn't crafts inside. It was a nameplate that read "Got Milk, Owner: Stephanie Rose Moscove." At first Stephanie didn't quite realize the implications of the gift. Then it turned into a moment mother and daughter will remember for the rest of their lives.

Laura says that "in my whole life, I have never seen my daughter light up like that." And she jokes, "my neck still hurts from the hug I got, but it was worth every chiropractic visit."

For one little girl who was ready to give up riding, meeting a rock star changed her life.

⟶ OLIVIER

He's known he was special since the day he was born. A stunning colt with, as Madeleine Austin, his breeder/owner put it, "expensive markings—four white socks and a blaze" he has a personality to match his vibrant looks.

When Liz Austin, Madeleine's daughter, first met Olivier, she wasn't really thinking that this would be her horse. Liz' horse American Pie had been her "once in a lifetime" love. This horse, she thought, would be her mom's.

Madeleine had bred Rowillie, her mare, to Idocus, an amazing stallion that she greatly admired. Rowillie was her foundation broodmare, producing a lot of nice babies. But, no doubt about it, Olivier was the nicest baby she had seen.

As a yearling, Olivier was the highest rated Dutch Warmblood in North America in his age group. Head inspector Geet van der Veen recommended they keep him a stallion. They followed the advice.

At four, Olivier went to the 100 day testing for breeding stallions in California. There he earned the highest scores of any stallion for movement in the long test: eights or higher across the board.

As he grew up, Madeleine rode and trained him, and Liz, as she grew, sometimes worked with him too. Truth to tell, she didn't much like him. He was a big, strong stallion and she had never ridden stallions before. She first rode him when he was three and she was 16. It wasn't a good match. Liz says they "butted heads." But, she had to admit, he had "spectacular presence."

Then Liz got the ride on another stallion: Hero. She started to get a feel for how to ride a stallion. You have to, "stroke their egos."

she says. She showed Hero in the Young Riders, doing very well with him, really clicking.

Meanwhile, Olivier went to stay with Pierre St. Jacques for a year, for training. He also entered his first competition. He won.

In 2003 Olivier returned home. He was seven. It had become more and more apparent that he was an international calibre horse. He had, as Elizabeth says, "the whole package—movement, temperament, looks." And personality. Liz soon nicknamed him "Fizzy" after a Muppets character who was rather mouthy.

But Madeleine didn't need an international horse. The horse had more talent than she needed. She encouraged Liz to take the ride. If Liz didn't show him, they might as well sell him to someone who would encourage his talents.

So Liz headed to Florida to work with Jen Baumert, taking both stallions with her. From Florida she would call her mom to tell her how she was doing. In the beginning, it was all about Hero. But things shifted. Over time, it was less and less about Hero; more about Fizzy.

Fizzy's character had captured her as well as his talent. Liz would walk into the barn in the morning and whistle. Fizzy would answer her with a scream. The partnership that had started so rockily grew and became stronger. Fizzy would do something well and Liz would tell him, "you're a superstar."

"Well, if you think *that's* good," Fizzy would say, then let me show you *this.*

Fizzy learned many tricks to get yet even more attention. Complete adoration obviously is to Fizzy the only acceptable form of attention. Liz bought him a squeaky toy and he was quite proud of himself when he learned what to do with it. Now if he is in his stall and wants attention, he picks up his squeaky toy and –squeaks it. His ears prick forward as he looks at you as if to say "Is this cute or what?"

When Liz returned north, she and Fizzy were doing Third Level. Feeling that many young horses are pushed too fast and too hard, Liz took things slowly with Fizzy. The most important thing for her was for her horse to be happy and confident.

Liz says, "he makes me smile every day, he's so much fun. The feeling I get when I ride him makes my eyes light up."

When Fizzy was nine, Liz became a working student for Lendon Gray. Gray loved the horse. Despite Liz' youth and lack of experience, she told her, "You can't decide when you get your great horse. When you get him or her you go for it."

Liz took Fizzy to Gray's Youth Dressage Festival, where they competed at the Prix St. Georges Level. The pair performed a clean sweep of their classes, winning the test with a 69, while Liz won the equitation class (scoring 92) and the written test (with a 90). It was, Liz says, "a great weekend!"

Liz didn't compete Fizzy in Young Rider competitions because she wanted him to progress at his own pace. Besides, they had international goals in mind!

When the Brentina Cup was announced, it fit right in with the track Liz and Olivier were on. The program was created for up and coming riders from 18-26 who were not ready to be professionals yet. The idea was to shine a light on riders who would be the future of the sport, to make sure they didn't get lost by competing with the Debbies and Tunys and Stefans!

Qualifiers for the cup would be held at designated shows, among them Ox Ridge, Saratoga, and Westbrook. Two "S" judges would officiate. Competing at Intermediaire II level, riders would need at least a 60% average from two shows to qualify for the finals.

Liz had no expectations for the event. With little funding behind her (Fizzy paid his way to the qualifiers through his breeding fees) she had little experience showing at that level. Yet she got a 62% at the first qualifier. The judges felt like their test had been too conservative, too underridden.

Liz wasn't about to let that happen again. She knew what Fizzy was capable of and that it was only she who determined how high he could go. She stepped up to the plate, let out the stops and the pair won the next qualifier with a 68 %. She and Fizzy ended up with the number one qualifying average in the nation.

And, as Liz says, he "came out with a smile on his face every time."

Now they were qualified for Gladstone, on their way to the Brentina Cup!

That was when Liz started feeling sick. She was exhausted, totally drained. A friend told her she might have mono. No, she insisted, she couldn't. It was just a flu or something passing.

A visit to the doctor proved the friend was right. She had mono.

She couldn't ride, she was so drained, so sick. But she was qualified, what was she going to do? Her mom stepped in and rode Fizzy, keeping him ready so if Liz recovered enough at least he would be fit.

It wasn't until the last possible moment that she could leave and still make it to Gladstone that Liz decided she could go. And that was when she discovered how far they had come.

This horse that she "butted heads with," this horse that she didn't want to ride, gave his all for her. He was "a genius, just amazing." He "carried me through the test."

Coming out, Liz was in tears, it had been such a lovely test. Lovely, she knew, because of Fizzy. Even Klaus Balkenhol, who was watching, said, "It looked as though he were a schoolmaster and you were just learning on him."

The judges were judging Fizzy, not his feverishly ill passenger. Five international judges gave them a score averaged to 70.39 %, the winning score.

In the victory gallop, Liz rode the horse she had known since birth. The announcer, in acknowledgement of what a family collaboration this victory had been, played "We are Family," as the horses circled the Gladstone arena.

TEACHERS

⤵ Antigua

Will Faudree has spent his life working with horses. Green horses: some off the track, some just young and green. Although he loved eventing, he had never had an upper level horse.

When he began training with Philip Dutton, Philip told him, "if this is what you really want to do, then you need a horse that can teach you."

And, Philip added, "I know the perfect horse, but I don't think the woman will sell him."

Philip made the call anyways. Much to his surprise, the woman said yes, she was willing to sell. She was in the process of building a house, and she needed the money.

So Will found himself on a plane to Australia, accompanied by Philip's head groom Colby Saddington. Colby had seen the horse before, when she and Philip were in Sydney for the 2000 Olympics.

It was a long way to look at a horse, and when Will first saw Antigua, he was distinctly unimpressed. He didn't seem worth the trip. The horse was small, barely 16 hands, and would hardly catch your eye. A sunbleached coat and long mane covered a fat, out of shape horse. His expression as he stood tied to a trailer, was bored: "ho hum, just another day at the job." He didn't seem to have much personality either.

However, when Will got on him, his feelings changed. When he put his leg on the horse, the horse moved right off. He put his head down, he did flying changes. This horse was a solid citizen. The horse had been ridden to the four star level, so he had the experience that Will needed.

Colby took a video of Will riding, and they returned home to Philip's farm in West Grove, Pennsylvania to let him take a look at it. Will's mother asked Philip if he thought Will could ride the horse.

Philip retorted, "A monkey could, so Will's got half a chance."

So Antigua (Brad) came to live in America with Will Faudree.

For their first competition, they did Preliminary. For their second, they moved right up to Advanced, competing at Pine Top in Georgia.

They aced the dressage, scoring a 35, and went clean cross country. Show jumping saw one rail fall. They were quickly developing a very close relationship, a genuine partnership. Brad was teaching Will how to ride a cross-country course. As they went on course, Will could feel Brad thinking "I know exactly why I'm here for this kid."

Will teaches a lot of clinics and people constantly ask him "How do you learn to ride cross-country?" Although Will is quick to credit the great instructors he's had in his life, he says, "The one who has taught me the most is Antigua. He's my coach."

He's also a real character, a "sucker for attention." His whole goal in life, Will says, is "to meet Mrs. Pastures."

While he's on the job, though, Brad takes it very seriously. When you put his tack on, he knows it's time to work and he "gives 100 percent every time." Will says he has taught him so much about staying out of a horse's way. He has such a great work ethic and gets very angry when he doesn't get worked.

Riding him is "a dream. It's an honor to get on a horse like that every day. He's such an athlete." Antigua is "my best friend, he's like my big brother. I can't tell people the type of bond we have, he's my soulmate."

There is a saying: "Show me your horse and I'll show you who you are." It's so true, says Will, "we both like to be the center of attention."

In 2002, Will and Brad won the Markham Trophy at both the

Foxhall CCI 3 Star and the Fair Hill CCI for being the highest placed Young Rider.

The following year, they went to Kentucky for the Rolex Kentucky Three Day Event, Will's first four star. Walking the course was unnerving, it was massive!! Looking at the fences, Will realized "not just anybody can do this. Horse and rider need to have a real partnership." Will tackled his apprehension by riding very forward and Brad just took care of him. Brad taught him how important rideability is on a course of this size. His attitude was, "It's OK, Dad, I've got this," but "this is how you have to ride me on a course like this."

Brad always tries his hardest. He "struggles" in dressage and needs an "accurate, melodic ride over fences," but given that he will contort his body to not touch a jump. He's an "orangatuan" in the starting box, so excited that he's going to go cross country! Then at one minute to the start, he settles down, he and Will both zone in, and as their hearts beat together, they merge and become one being, ready to tackle the course.

Off of their performance at Rolex, Will, at only 21 years old, qualified for the Pan American Games, where he and Brad were part of the gold medal winning team. When they returned to Kentucky in 2004, their ride there helped them qualify for the Athens Olympics, where they went as the reserve rider. In 2005 they completed Badminton, and were second at Fair Hill in the fall.

In 2006 they had their best Kentucky yet, with a clean show jumping round, a real milestone since that phase has proven to be their Achilles heel. This qualified them for the World Equestrian Games in Aachen, Germany. Not only was the qualification remarkable, but Will scored another triumph out of the occasion.

Christine Bates and her husband, from Australia, had known Brad before Will purchased him. They came to visit him in the barn at Rolex. "Oh my God, he is so different," they told Will. "He used to be so quiet, so dull." They were amazed at the inquisitive and outgoing horse that now poked his nose out of the stall.

At the World Equestrian Games, the American team unfortunately missed the Bronze medal by a heartbreaking two tenths of a point. Will and Brad came 19th individually.

Going to the World Equestrian Games was "surreal. You can't treat it like just another event."

It is the single greatest honor for an athlete to be able to represent his country in international competition. Because of Brad, Will has been fortunate enough to do it three times. Brad has given him a tremendous foundation.

Brad "bails him out." At the Worlds, Brad and Will were approaching a bank bounce uphill. It was followed by a skinny going downhill. Will got Brad in wrong, he hung a leg and nearly went over. Will says, "In slow motion, it was incredible. We were straight up and down with me wrapped around his neck." Yet somehow, Brad got Will "back in the tack" and they continued.

Will's human foundation has been Bobo Rowe and Kathleen Zins in Texas, where he grew up, Karen and David O'Connor, his coaches as a Young Rider, Philip Dutton, whom he was based with for three years, and Bobby Costello, who is "adamant about tedious details."

Now based in his own place in Southern Pines, Will says Bobby has made a big impact on his jumping. Mark Phillips has been a major factor in his success at the international level.

Will takes what he's learned from Antigua and applies it to his other horses. He is "the horse that made me. He's an amazing partner, horse, athlete and friend." Will says "you wait your whole life, you dream from the time you can speak, of going to the Olympics, to Worlds, and all of a sudden you have this horse and you get there."

You work hard and "sometimes it works and sometimes it doesn't." Will couldn't believe he was at Worlds. Although he certainly wanted to do his personal best at an event like that, he felt he didn't achieve that because he was so overwhelmed just being there. "It's a learning experience, a learning curve" he says.

He has the utmost respect for Brad and feels like he held him back from what he was capable of. Brad could have been a medal winning horse at the Olympics or Worlds, but wasn't, Will feels, because of his own inexperience.

This year (2007) at Kentucky was the cross country ride of Will's life. Unfortunately Brad threw a shoe and stepped on the clip so he had to be withdrawn. Will felt that during the round, Brad was giving him a cross country lesson. His thoughts were verified, when, after the round, a woman came up to him and said, "I want you to know that your round was a lesson on how to ride cross country."

There is no doubt that this is a partnership that was meant to be. For Will, Brad has taught him all about riding at the upper levels, about accepting nothing less than the best. Brad has gained a best friend. He has come out of his shell, grown from a withdrawn horse that hid at the back of his stall to being the first one with his head out, wanting to be the center of attention and begging for treats. Brad is "a phenomenal animal." And for Will Faudree there is nothing better than walking into the barn, seeing Brad stick his head out of the stall, and ask, "So what are we doing today, dad?"

⇁ Impy

Nina hated the horse. Ok, well maybe that was a little too strong a word, but she sure didn't like him. He was mean. As she stood at the mounting block, helping the kids in the therapeutic program mount and dismount, he would turn his head around and try to bite her. He was little, too, pony-sized although he was a full blooded Morgan. He was plain brown with a little white swirl on his face. Besides being mean, he didn't look like much.

And he had rules, too. They were simple rules. If he wasn't fed first, he would kick the barn down.

If he was turned out first, he would charge up and down the fence line screaming and throwing a temper tantrum worthy of any two year old child, creating so much ruckus that everyone would cave and he would get his way. He was never turned out first; he was always turned out second. He had to be the second horse brought in, as well. If he was brought in first and found himself alone in the barn he would simply pulverize his stall.

Impy had everyone over a barrel and he knew it. For despite his quirks, he was a great therapy horse. So things were done according to Impy's rules.

Impy (Snow's Imperial) was bred and born at Snow's Morgan Farm in northern New Jersey. After a career as a show horse, he found a second career as a trail mount for his new owner, Pat Cirkus. When she founded the Milford Center for Therapeutic Riding, Impy found himself with yet another job.

Then Impy's owners got divorced. Pat needed a home for Impy, and asked if he could come board with Nina at Whisper Wind Farm. Nina said yes. What she didn't tell Pat was that Impy would not run her barn the way he ran Pat's. When Impy came to Nina's barn he would live by Nina's rules.

Impy was 24 by now and rather set in his ways. He wasn't open to change, but that was too bad, because life is about changes. His life with Pat had been rather leisurely, going on an occasional trail ride, doing light duty with the kids in the therapeutic program. But break time was over. Whisper Wind is a working farm and Impy was going to have to do his share.

Nina soon discovered that Impy's interpretation of "the rules" were a simple matter of misunderstanding. They had never been correctly explained to him. When Impy ran around screaming the first time he was turned out alone, Nina went out in the paddock with him. She went up to him, held his halter, and said firmly "We don't do that here."

Impy was a bit taken aback, but he got the message.

At Pat's, Impy had been so fresh that he would throw a temper tantrum when he wasn't fed first. That changed fast. Now he was working too hard. Temper tantrum? Who had the energy for that?

It didn't take long at all for Impy to learn to live by Nina's rules. Along the way, Nina's opinion of him changed drastically. Impy had become an incomparable lesson horse.

He learned to jump for the first time, and loved it. He would never stop and would jump from any distance, any angle a rider placed him at. His small ears would continuously point forward as though to say "What can I do for you? How can I please you?"

Nina's daughter, Camille, grew to love riding Impy. When Camille's pony died, Impy became her stand in. He did the job well. Camille fell in love.

One day Nina received a heartbreaking phone call from Pat. She was dying. Nina would be receiving Impy's papers in the mail. Impy was Pat's only dependent, and she wanted to ensure that he was left with a good home.

Nina sent Pat a photo of Impy and Camille kissing. The photo remained on Pat's nightstand until the day she died.

Impy takes Camille fox hunting, goes out on trail rides, and runs the gamut from taking little kids over their first cross rails to winning jumper championships with Camille (he was the Tri-County Jumper Champion of the Year in the New York area where Whisper Wind is based.) Nina knows she can trust him with anyone.

At 31, Impy colicked very badly. Rushed to the hospital, Nina was told that the vets weren't sure if he would make it. He was too old to risk surgery. Nina knew one thing for sure: they would do whatever they could to save him. Impy had never been sick, he had always paid his way, and Camille loved the little brown horse. Impy had to have the chance.

It paid off. After 72 hours of hospitalization and IV fluids, Impy was out of the woods. He recovered beautifully, and, once again, he and Camille are tearing around the jumper courses. The little energizer bunny is back.

Nina has to give Impy credit. He proved her wrong. The horse she "hated" she now can't say enough good things about. Impy is wonderful, irreplaceable. He takes care of her students, of her daughter.

Impy, she says, is "the best. "

➙ MAC

He is a Tennesee Walking Horse, sired by World Grand Champion Pride's Final Edition. He's big, black and beautiful. But he was also BAAADDD. At only six years old, Mac (Final's Back in Black) had already lived in five different states, gone through three sales and had had nine owners.

She had decided it was time to quit riding. Because of a bad back, sitting on a horse was just too painful.

But that didn't mean she didn't want to have any horses. Carol Ross and her husband had a small farm: 15 acres of open land. It was a lot to mow. Carol thought, "why not just get some horses and they can graze it for us?" She told her husband, "I could just put up an electric fence and put some horses on it."

He didn't answer. Carol's interpretation of his silence was "Go ahead, honey." So she did. She bought an Appaloosa out of the circular *Steed Read*. It was dead lame. In a short period of time, six horses, a donkey and a pony were "mowing the lawn."

But soon just watching the horses wasn't enough for Carol. She began riding the retirees at a walk around the perimeter of the farm. Of course, that only whetted her appetite. She wanted to ride. And she could ride, even with her aching back, if she got a gaited horse.

Mac was the first one she looked at. He was skinny, at only 900 pounds skinnier in fact than any horse Carol had ever seen. Not only did he have no fat, he had no muscle. He was also scared, so scared that he was downright dangerous. Carol's heart went out to him. She didn't even bother to ride him; she knew she had to save him.

When he was delivered a few days later, he was wearing a trail bridle that had been on his head for over two years. The former owners suggested that Carol leave it on. "He can be a little hard to catch and a little head shy," they explained. The extent of their underestimation was enormous.

When the vet tried to do a pre-purchase exam, Mac kicked the vet in the kneecap, putting her out of commission and ending the exam prematurely.

Carol, ignoring the former owner's advice, took the trail bridle off. It took her three and a half weeks to get a halter on him. Touching his ear was downright impossible. The first time she went in his stall, he threw himself against the back wall, shaking like a leaf. When she approached him, saying, "You poor thing, what on earth are you so afraid of?" he bolted around the stall. Carol doesn't even know how she made it out of there.

Carol did some research, speaking to most of his former owners, trying to find out what could have made the horse so frightened and defensive. Basically she was told he was just a "bad" horse. And while she was told that, Mac was doing everything he could to prove it.

He kicked her in the chest, he bit her (taking a good chunk out of her arm), he reared, and he bolted. He knocked her down and ran her over. If she was behind him or tried to brush his tail, he kicked. If she tried to touch his head or ears he would bite. In fact, the only area on his body that she could touch was the saddle area.

In the first year she owned him, Carol only tried to ride him six times. One day when she took him on a trail ride, he bolted. She didn't think he would ever stop. He just ran and ran and ran. Luckily it was on an old railroad bed so the path was straight. Carol thought to herself, "I wonder how this is going to end."

"What are you going to do?" her husband asked her one day. And he, Carol admits, didn't know half of what Mac had done to her.

Carol had just heard about Natural Horsemanship and hoped

33

that these teachings could save her new horse. She'd tried everything else. It was his last chance. She believed that he wasn't mean or bad—just very scared. Everyone kept telling her to get rid of him, that if she didn't he would kill her. Either this worked, or Carol was going to have to do what was safest for the people around him and fairest to him: put him down.

Carol began going to every Natural Horsemanship clinic she could find. Then she began hosting them herself so she could invite the best teachers she could find. She ended up hosting as many as eight clinics a year. Along the way, the knowledge she gained transformed Mac and transformed her life.

Carol now calls Mac the "Natural Horsemanship Ambassador." The horse whose ear couldn't be touched now can be led by his ear. Mac, who wouldn't do anything Carol asked, now does whatever she requests, and never says no. The bond between them is unmistakable. Without him, Carol says she "would be nothing more than an unknown voice" trying to convince people to deal gently with their horses and to communicate in a way they can understand. Because of Mac and his reputation, they have been able to change lives. Mac has brought hope to people and horses. There is help available: "bad" horses just need good training. As Carol says, "he's the motivator, not me."

Watching him at liberty—walking over bridges, through spaces between barrels barely large enough to accommodate him, and squeezing under low hanging ropes—while Carol signals him with subtle cues on the ground—makes it hard to believe that anyone ever had a problem with this horse.

Looking at where Mac came from and where he is now convinces people that there is a better way. Once people understand the concept, and how it works they look at horses in an entirely different way.

Carol and Mac have done demonstrations for all types of equine groups as well as benefits and fund raisers. Whether it's hunter/jumper, dressage, pony club, draft, or therapeutic riding barns, Mac makes an impression. People can't help but fall in love with the stunning black horse. He has been nicknamed Mac the Wonder Horse.

Recently, Carol was attending a weekend Natural Horsemanship event at the Big E in West Springfield, Massachusetts. Sitting in the audience, she was spotted by passersby. At least 30 attendees came to her to thank her and Mac for inspiring them to learn more about their horse's nature, for the relationship they and their horse now have, and for helping them stay safe with their horses. They told her stories of how seeing her with Mac changed their life. "We are here today because of you and Mac," she heard over and over again.

Carol's bad back led her to Mac. Mac led her to a whole new life. She feels that he came to her to teach her to build confidence in people and help them build confidence in their horses. Mac started it all. He has never won a World Championship, but he's done a lot to change the world.

⤴ Platinum Plus

On a good day his name is Platinum Plus. On a bad day it's Platypus Plow.

Sharon Santandra-Juerrs was ready to make the move to Preliminary Level eventing and she wanted a horse that could take her there. She needed one with experience, one who had done it all and could teach her the ropes.

Sharon had had several other horses, but she never progressed the way she'd hoped to. She'd get stuck at novice or training level. Sometimes it was a soundness problem; some of her horses just wouldn't jump certain fences. She wanted that one special horse to help her fulfill her dream.

Like many New Yorkers, Sharon's father spent the winter in Florida. It was February, so Sharon decided that it would be a good time to visit her father, escape the cold and do some horse hunting. At one farm she tried a nice chestnut. She liked him a lot. But Sharon worked for an equine veterinarian, and she had learned a good deal about conformation. She didn't like the horse's legs: they were crooked, and the horse paddled in front. So she passed him up.

She tried a horse at another farm, and wasn't particularly impressed.

There *was* another horse at the farm that she could look at, she was told. As long as she was here, Sharon figured, why not? She asked them to bring him out. When the horse came out all Sharon could think was, "*That's* the horse???"

He was ugly. He was the *last* horse Sharon would ever consider.

A big boned, scrawny gray, with a high head set on the end of a skinny neck. Definitely not Sharon's prototype. Sharon's ideal horse was the classic Thoroughbred: pretty, balanced, with a beautiful head set at the end of a long, elegant neck And bay. Her horses *had* to be bay.

This horse would never do. No way. This horse would be at the bottom of her list, of anyone's list.

Not only was he ugly, he didn't even have that much experience, and he had certainly never seen a Preliminary fence. He'd competed at novice, or possibly one Training Level event. He was six years old, a Dutch Warmblood/Thoroughbred cross. Or so Sharon was told. She personally didn't see any evidence of Thoroughbred blood in the geeky gelding.

"Toby" had been raised in Florida, and was owned by a 16 year old girl. He had spent a few months in training with Ralph Hill. Sara, his owner, was downsizing so Toby had to find a new home.

Ugly or not, Sharon was here, so she might as well try the horse. She rode him, and says his trot was "goddawful!" But he was a willing and honest jumper.

Her stepmother liked Toby and pointed out that "A kid rides him. If a kid can ride him, you can ride him."

"Thanks a lot," thought Sharon.

Sharon left Florida and flew back to New York. On the trip, she did a lot of thinking. The gray horse kept running through her mind. She decided she needed to take another look at him.

Two weeks later, Sharon went back to try Toby again. She asked Sara if she could ride the horse cross country. Sara was very helpful and let her try any tests she wanted with Toby. Sharon was terrified of ditches, yet Toby sailed over them like Pegasus. And when she took him on a trail ride, he was rock solid. Traffic, including Mack trucks, rushed by. Toby didn't flinch. "That," said Sharon, "was when I knew this was it. This was the horse I was looking for."

Back home again, Sharon completed all the paperwork to make

Toby hers, and made arrangements to have him shipped to a nearby barn, the Southlands Foundation.

Once Toby arrived, Sharon couldn't wait to go pick him up. She pulled up to Southlands and went looking for her new horse. Although only a few weeks had passed since she had seen him, she couldn't find him. She was at the stall where he was supposed to be, but he wasn't there. She was confused. A grey plow horse was in the stall!

"That can't be my horse," she thought. "I wouldn't buy such an ugly horse."

So she announced to the barn: "That's not my horse!"

But, she was assured, it *was* her horse. The long trip north from Florida had not been kind to Toby. Big boned horses are particularly unsightly without meat on those bones, and Toby had dropped weight on the trip.

OK, he was ugly and he was skinny, but he *was* her horse. Sharon went home with Toby.

It didn't take long for Sharon to remember why she had purchased him. His athleticism and honesty became more and more apparent. He wasn't easy, but he loved to jump and his ability inspired confidence in Sharon. Fences that were downright scary from the ground were not so bad from Toby's back. As Sharon says, "He just takes you, he just goes, it's riding at a whole different level."

Toby was athletic in another way too, bucking when Sharon got tight, letting her know it was time to loosen up. Sharon had to develop her rodeo skills, learning to stick to her horse.

Sharon trains her own horses, attending a lot of clinics with riders like Michael Page, Denny Emerson and Dee Dee Cook to fine tune her skills. At home she often works with Don Patterson. She also gets tips from fellow event riders, whom she finds very supportive: "everybody is very helpful and encouraging."

A hunter/jumper rider for most of her life, Sharon developed a mental strategy to deal with cross-country fences that would otherwise have proven too intimidating. Nothing in the ring scared her, she was used to those. So she simply translated cross-country fences into their ring equivalents. An oxer is still an oxer whether it is composed of white poles or tree branches. A bench with a rail on it is nothing more than an oxer. A table? Just a square oxer. A big tree across the track? It's nothing more than a vertical. I've done that, so I can do this. The technique built Sharon's confidence because she could look at everything and think, no problem, I know how to do that.

Over time, Toby's geeky appearance transformed. The nerd on the beach transformed into the muscled strong man. His personality blossomed, too. Sharon learned that his favorite treat is Swedish Fish—open a pack and "he's on you like a hounddog." Toby became a real people horse, and loved to play, particularly with Sharon's nephews.

Sharon says that when he's relaxed, "he still looks like a pony," but when he's competing, he "grows into his own personality, he becomes 17 hands."

At first, Sharon had to retreat once again to Novice Level events. They both needed the experience, as well as the chance to get acquainted and figure each other out in competition. Then they advanced to Training, but Sharon's eye was always on Preliminary. That was her goal, her dream, and she knew Toby would take her there.

Their first Preliminary, Sharon decided, would be at Groton.

The reaction was predictable. "Groton?" people asked. "Are you crazy??? That's such a hard course."

But Sharon felt comfortable at Groton. She had always enjoyed competing there, so that was where she wanted to make her Preliminary Level debut.

But first things, first. Sharon had to find out if she and Toby could manage that height. Attending a nearby HITS (Horse Shows in the Sun) event, they entered a jumper class where the fences were 3'6". (The maximum height for a Preliminary Level fence is 3'7") Things didn't go quite as planned when Sharon went off course. The judge kept blowing the whistle to let Sharon know she was eliminated. Sharon kept going. She and Toby were thrown out of the ring.

Ok, so that wasn't quite the practice Sharon had had in mind. She entered another class, a bigger one. These fences were set at 3'9". They were big—but not to Toby. He sailed around the course, leaving no doubt in Sharon's mind as to his ability. Sharon says, "It's so nice to be able to trust a horse like this."

The mishap over the class worked in their favor. By jumping a bigger course than she would have to do at Groton the actual obstacles she and Toby would have to face shrunk in comparison.

The time had come to tackle Preliminary. Entries were sent in, the trailer was packed, and finally they were on their way to Groton. Very excited and very nervous, Sharon kept talking to herself and to Toby—"You can do this—we can do this."

When they arrived Sharon settled Toby into his stall. Then she went out to walk the cross-country course. Then she walked it again. And again.

"Where is Sharon?" people would ask.

"She's walking the course" someone would answer.

"Have you seen Sharon?"

"She's walking the course again."

"I think I walked the course, oh, about 500 times," she says.

The course was *big*.

There was a water jump, there were Sharon's bugaboos—the ditches—there were steps and coffins. The oxers were so wide, Sharon says, that she had to stop looking at them. If she spotted one, panic would begin to set in. So she would just turn away and say, "Nope, I'm not going to look at them."

As she came to one huge, "big mama oxer" Bobby Costello, with whom she was walking the course, warned her "Don't ride backwards to this one!"

The first phase, dressage, is not Sharon, or Toby's favorite part of an event. Sitting to Toby's trot is a bit of an exercise in masochism. And then there's the test, "too disciplined" for Sharon's taste. Never one to waste time or energy learning dressage tests, Sharon crammed for it the night before. Predictably, the test was "so-so. We always finish somewhere in the middle of the pack."

Next up was the long awaited, big moment: a Preliminary Level cross-country course. After so many years, so many horses, so many disappointments, Sharon's dream was about to happen.

Sharon's nerves were also on edge. After finishing their warm-up, she took Toby to a quiet spot where they could breathe and relax. Then it was into the start box.

"Where is the porta-potty?" Sharon wondered. She was so nervous she felt sick. Sick but excited, because she knew Toby could do this.

Nerves were left behind as they burst out of the start box. Nothing remained but Sharon, Toby and the course. "You just get into it," Sharon says. "You're not aware of anything else but your connection with your horse and the course."

Toby was "awesome. He just flew over everything. I wish everyone could have a horse like him." Of course, when they came to the oxer where Sharon had been told not to ride backwards on the approach, she "rode backwards." Toby responded with a big buck on the other side to let Sharon know she had failed her part of the job. Sharon got the point. "OK, you're in control now dude," she told him. Toby settled into a nice hunter rhythm and the rest of the course was magic.

Finishing the course was "A high like you've never experienced in your life. It just can't be matched. You've done it!" Not only had they done it, but they'd done it well, as Sharon says, "clean, pretty and honest."

Toby came off the course "proud, he knew he'd been good!"

Their cross country round moved them up from their midpack

dressage placing to ninth overall. Now one phase remained, the stadium jumping.

The course started easy, with a smooth flow. But as they approached the middle things got tougher. There was a short turn to a big triple combination, a turn that tripped up quite a few competitors. As Sharon made the turn, she wasn't really concentrating on the course. Still on a cross country high, still amazed that she and Toby had just completed their first Preliminary course, her feeling about the stadium was "Let's just get this over with."

Luckily, the other half of the partnership *was* focused on the course. He came around the corner, honed in on the big triple combination, and waited for his mom to ask him to jump. She never asked. Toby jumped in and as Sharon says, "saved my butt. I shouldn't have been taking a nap in the middle of the course." But her lack of guidance caused them to take a rail down.

Despite the untimely nap, the stadium course wasn't all that difficult. Many of their "practice" rounds at horse shows had been much trickier. Sharon was pleased.

Luckily, the rail didn't cost them a spot and they finished in ninth place.

Sharon and Toby worked and trained together toward a goal and they both grew through that training and through their bond with each other. Doing Preliminary had been Sharon's dream and Toby "nailed it for me." The geeky looking horse at the bottom of her list became the one she couldn't live without. After kissing all the frogs, Sharon had found her prince.

Humans Helping
Horses

⌐᠊ᴑ Eli

A lot of us say it. "Horses are my life." And we mean it. In a way.

Then there was Eli.

Eli started working on the racetrack as a young man, a boy some would say. He started at the bottom, doing whatever needed to be done. Mucking stalls, feeding, rubbing the young Thoroughbreds to that slick shine. He did it all. He hot walked, and was an exercise rider. He was even an assistant trainer for a while.

Eli lived at the track. Racetracks provide housing for some of their help, dormitories that are often located above the barns, and sometimes found as stand alone housing. These dorms were Eli's home. He travelled from racetrack to racetrack, job to job. When the horses moved, so did Eli.

The dorms were free for the grooms: no charge for rent, for electricty, for heat. Some of them included air conditioning. And there were kitchens on the track, kitchens where the help go to eat.

Eli loved to gamble, and could often be found at the betting windows located for the help in the kitchens. When he wasn't taking care of his equine charges, he was betting on them.

Everyone knew Eli, at least in passing. He was there every day, a fixture on the track. And as one generation gave way to the next, Eli was still there. In fact, when that generation gave way to the next, Eli was still there.

Eli spent his entire adult life on the backside of a racetrack. When he got to be too old to do most jobs, trainers at Laurel Racetrack in Maryland would always find something for him to do. There were chores that Eli could still manage so he could earn enough to eat, to survive. By this point it took Eli about half an hour to walk from the bunkhouse to the barn, and probably the same amount of time for him to walk a horse around the shedrow once.

But he kept going, and the trainers kept helping him.

When Eli died, it was estimated that he was about 103. He had spent approximately 85 years taking care of horses on the track.

He never rubbed a triple crown winner and no one presented him with a gold watch for his years of service, but his legacy was a life of service—to horses.

⟶ Locket's Meadow

Just two horses. That was all Kathleen and her husband planned to keep on their new farm. Kathleen had heard and read about the plight of PMU foals (foals that result from breeding mares to produce urine for the replacement hormone industry), and had always wanted to help, but she had had nowhere to put the foals. Now that they had a farm, she couldn't wait to do her part.

By doing a lot of research, Kathleen learned the truth about the business that produces Premarin and Prempro. It is nothing short of torture for horses. Mares are bred and then kept in stalls for six or seven months at a time while their urine is collected for use in the drug. Horses, who are bred to roam free, are confined with no ability to move. It was a horrifying scenario, and Kathleen was glad she now had the opportunity to help.

Although her husband David didn't quite share her enthusiasm, Kathleen had calmed his fears by telling him that they would only adopt two horses. He thought he could handle that.

While doing her research, Kathleen had discovered that foals were available for adoption on websites. In fact, Kathleen discovered that there was a whole underground railroad of people helping the PMU horses on the web.

The first foal that Kathleen found to adopt was a small, very pink Appaloosa named Benny. But when she went to go ahead with the adoption procedure, she discovered that other people already had claimed him. "Too bad," she thought, "he was really cute."

Later, she checked the site again, and found that Benny was no longer reserved. It turned out that two women had been planning to adopt him, but when their husbands found out, the plan was voted down.

So now Kathleen had Benny, but of course she wouldn't dream of raising one foal all alone. She continued to look on the website. There were only two foals left. One was blurry and one was but a flash of light. So Kathleen did the only logical thing. She tossed a coin. The blurry photo won.

However, there was a catch. The farmer refused to sell the foal in the blurry photo. He told Kathleen that the foal, a light breed colt, had crooked legs. Kathleen begged him to reconsider, knowing that the foal was doomed to slaughter if she didn't get him. But the man wouldn't budge.

I'll send you another one just like him, the man promised. Kathleen had no choice.

There was that one extra foal, one no one had adopted. Although Kathleen had promised David that only two horses would come home, she could foster the extra foal, couldn't she? No harm in that!

So three foals, each a little over four months old, arrived at Locket's Meadow. Bart, the foster foal, was smart and sweet. Too smart for David, it proved. In less than two days of his arrival, he had walked up to David and put his head on his shoulder.

"How could we let anyone else have him?" David asked. That was easy. Bart was home to stay.

Beatrice was another story. The "light breed colt" arrived as a draft filly. The huge pinto did have a medicine hat, but that was the only resemblance she bore to the colt with the crooked legs that Kathleen had originally intended to give a home.

And she was not sweet. She was angry, very angry. Beatrice had been weaned from her mother much too early. She was furious at what people had done, and she wanted her mom back. She was, in fact, scary. She would swing her haunches at you, kick, buck, try to jump out of her paddock, and refuse to let anyone touch her. These tactics, coming from such a massive horse, were quite intimidating.

Bea's anti-social behavior didn't stop Kathleen. Her whole life she had wanted a horse. Now, at 39 she had gotten her first one (Well, her first three . . .) She was going to enjoy her dream and she was determined to give Beatrice a good life. And she had speed on her side. Being young and quick, Bea never managed to get her.

Of course, the horse population didn't come to an end with the three foals. Foals came to the farm to be adopted out. Some actually were. (Kathleen cries whenever one is adopted. They are, after all, her "children.") But most, well, you couldn't help but fall in love with them. So they stayed. The "one" horse she had dreamed of her whole life soon developed into an avalanche.

The "avalanche" has resulted in a home with over 20 horses. It's a lot of work, "overwhelming" Kathleen admits. But she does it because she can. How many people have the room or the time to adopt all these horses? Or have a husband, who is, "a saint?"

Although initially David struggled with all the changes the horses brought about, he has now accepted it and relaxed into his new life. He has grown to love them.

Kathleen is quick to point out that, contrary to what some people think, these are not "junk" horses. The foals she first adopted, now four years old, are lesson horses, troopers that she can put five year old kids on for a first lesson.

A nearby horse show, St. Peter's Charity Horse Show, managed by United States Equestrian Federation Steward Cynthia Jensen, now offers classes just for PMU horses. The point is to educate people about PMUs, to show that these horses are not throwaways. They are, "so amazing," Kathleen says, there are pintos, Quarter Horses, Appaloosas, and drafts. The classes help spectators understand that these are useful, adoptable horses. Of course they could (and do) compete in regular classes, but then people would not realize that they are PMU horses!

As demand for Premarin died down (not just from the work of educators like Kathleen, but also from the medical reports of extremely serious side effects from the drug, such as strokes, breast cancer, heart disease and deaths), the farms dropped from numbering in the hundreds to under 50. But farmers, with no more income to feed the horses, flooded the market with mares headed to the slaughterhouses. Again, rescuers moved in to save them.

The mares were more difficult to deal with than the foals. After being confined to their prisons for more than half a year, they had suffered terrible emotional wounds. There were big trust issues to work through. But Kathleen and David, and others like them, were willing to make the commitment to help these horses. Kathleen says, "We're very good at PMUs, we stay with it because we know that's what we're good at. We love them."

Both David and Kathleen have jobs besides the farm. They do not have a life besides the farm. But they wouldn't trade it for anything, as they both feel that "we're the luckiest people we know!"

Beatrice continued to be a challenge to Kathleen and David. The filly's anger was not lessening and she continued to act out. She was *great* with the foals: she mothered the new ones coming in. It was as if she felt that she needed to take the place of the mothers they had lost. But she couldn't continue to threaten the humans on the place.

One day Kathleen decided things had to change. She needed to have a talk with Beatrice. She snuck out of the house, thinking that she had escaped undetected by David. She went to Bea's stall, to where the filly stood eating her hay.

As soon as she saw Kathleen the filly stiffened. Her head raised, her body tensed.

Kathleen took a deep breath and began talking. "Beatrice," she said, "you don't have to be the Mommy. I'll do that. You're just a baby yourself."

Starting at her hip, Kathleen slowly worked her way up the filly's body towards her head.

As she made her way up talking in a soothing voice, Bea's head slowly began to drop and her body began to relax and lose its de-

49

fensive posture.

Kathleen continued speaking gently to Beatrice, and didn't notice when David snuck into the barn. Bea's nose was now nearly on the hay, and suddenly Kathleen realized that the hay was wet. "That's odd," she thought.

Then she looked at Beatrice's blue eyes. The filly was crying.

Kathleen burst into tears. David emerged from his hiding place. He, too, was crying.

From that moment on, Beatrice lost her anger. Although she is still the mommy to the other foals, and to the children that ride her, she is content to let Kathleen be *her* mommy. She understood Kathleen, and so let go of her fear and anger.

Beatrice (The Divine Miss Beatrice) is, Kathleen says, such a gift. Since that night she has been transformed. Kathleen now stands in awe of her. Bea understands the fears people have because she knows how it feels to feel lost and lonely and scared. She has grown so intuitive about those that ride her that she seems to know exactly what they need. She is the farm's therapeutic horse, and is particularly good with autistic kids. Bea is so perfect, so careful, and takes such good care of her charges.

One young rider at the barn had fallen off a horse while cantering and was so nervous that she hadn't cantered for years. She was given Bea for a lesson because the mare is so trustworthy.

The little girl was still scared, still nervous. Her instructor couldn't get the girl to do anything because of her fear. So Kathleen stepped in. "You have to trust me," she said. "This horse will not let anything happen to you."

She did trust Kathleen, and she did canter Bea. She was beaming. When Kathleen looked into the arena a short time later, she was jumping cross rails!

Kathleen and David founded Locket's Meadow to save one horse. Instead they have saved countless horses, found a whole new life of joy for themselves, and introduced hundreds to the gift of a horse.

For more information on Locket's Meadow, go to
www.locketsmeadow.com.

⟿ Hurricane

Horses, for people often seem to arrive in the form of angels. In return, the horses have their own angels. Debra Barlow is one such angel.

In 2004 and 2005, violent storms attacked throughout the world. Several of these storms, hurricanes of tremendous magnitude, struck the gulf coast of America, causing damage beyond anything the country had ever encountered, or could even imagine. Over **90,000** square miles of the south was declared a disaster zone.

The storms transformed several southern states into disaster areas, with more than a thousand human lives lost, and devastation as far—and beyond—as the eye could see. Rescue workers accustomed to devastation, men and women who had served in wars, been at earthquake sites, and were first responders to the Southeast Asian tsunami, people used to witnessing the worst that mother nature and man could offer, were in disbelief at the sights of the south.

Of course, it was not only humans that suffered. Animals of all types, sizes and breeds died or were injured. Lessons were learned about what to do and not do, in case of such a disaster.

In the case of horses, one thing became clear. Confinement meant death. With storm surges as high as 30 feet in some areas, any horse left in a barn drowned.

Horses left free often managed to make it to higher ground and survive. But, just surviving the storm, and the flooding, wasn't enough. What came next? What were they going to eat? What could they drink, besides the oily, muddy, foul water surrounding them after the flood? The water in some places was so foul that a cut or scrape that came in contact with it could mean dangerous, life threatening infection.

Debra Barlow runs Hopeful Haven Rescue in Shreveport, Louisiana. A sister organization, Rescue Ranch in Belle Chase is run by Lori Wilson. Lori had been injured prior to the hurricane and needed help and supplies for her rescue and for other horses that would be coming in after Hurricane Katrina.

Debra put together a convoy of 12 horse trailers full of supplies such as feed, hay, halters and medical supplies to take to Lori. She credits being able to put this together through the support of such organizations as the ASPCA, the Rhode Island SPCA, the Louisisana Humane Society, the United Christian Farm Workers, Best Friends (of Utah) and hundreds of smaller supporters from around the country.

Debra says "You just wouldn't believe what people will do. The generosity of people across the country is amazing."

Much of Louisiana was under martial law at the time. There were curfews and areas that no one was allowed into. But, because of Debra's work as an animal cruelty investigator (she was the team leader for the Northwest Louisiana VMA Horse Evacuation) with local police agencies, she had the necessary credentials.

The trailers were loaded up and ready to roll. Lori warned Debra that she would never be able to get through with the supplies. "They'll take your supplies," she told her.

"Not *my* supplies," thought Debra. They were going to go where they were meant to go! When Debra makes up her mind to do something, nothing is going to shake her off her path.

Debra had heard that supplies were being taken from people and then stockpiled, not getting through to the farmers and ranchers who needed food for their animals THAT DAY, not sometime in the future. Farmers would be put on a list one week and allowed to come get supplies the following week. But horses don't wait a week for food, they needed that food now!

Debra's convoy made it to the check point in Belle Chase. It was dark: 10:30 at night. Despite the late hour and the lack of light, the devastation was clear. It "looked like someone dropped a bomb." Debra was "floored, nothing will ever prepare you for something like that" she says. And it was the eeriest feeling, the dead silence. It gave Debra a sinking feeling in her stomach.

The convoy was stopped at this point by Sheriff Angie Sabastino. "I've been waiting for you all day," the Sheriff said.

She told Debra to follow her and for all the trailers to follow bumper to bumper. The convoy rolled on, stopping eventually at a "little rinky dink animal shelter."

"You're leaving the supplies here." the sheriff said.

"No," said Debra, "they're my supplies and I'm not leaving them here. They are going to Lori at Rescue Ranch."

Debra knew she had to reach Lori, but she also knew there was no cell phone reception in the area. Few towers were standing after the tremendous winds of the hurricane. She tried her cell phone anyways. No cell phone calls were going through. The one she made to Lori went through.

Debra unloaded some of her supplies at the animal shelter: 35 bales of hay and 25 bags of grain. It was a peace offering in a way, by giving them a little bit she would be able to deliver the rest with no trouble. Then the convoy rolled on—this time to Rescue Ranch.

The volunteers were physically exhausted and emotionally devastated from what they had seen that day. But they unloaded the 12 trailer's worth of supplies at their intended destination. Then they went to a nearby church where they spent the night.

Horses in Louisiana were often found mired in the marshes, and had to be pulled out. Some were pulled out by cowboys on horses, others by airboats. It was dangerous work. Often there was barbed wire lurking in the muddy water, wire that cut the horses and caused serious infections. These horses were another target for Debra, another group that needed the food she brought in.

For five months, every single weekend Debra and a devoted team of volunteers trucked food in to the devastated areas of Vermillion Parish. All in all, they brought in over 400 tons of feed and five 18 wheelers worth of hay and medical supplies.

Debra gives tremendous credit to her "elf" Lauren Gedaminski of Needham, Massachusetts, who worked the internet daily getting the much needed supplies and donations ready for the next convoys going out. Lauren worked endlessly toward hurricane relief and Debra says "my work couldn't have been done without her."

In order to know where best to direct her efforts, Debra had obtained a list of the hardest hit places from her friend Hank Moss. Hank and his brother Sonny owned a 700 acre spread in Erath and they had lost everything. Their 99 year old home was in ruins, with water marks on the walls at a height of 14 feet. Despite their loss, the brothers cheerfully pitched in to help the volunteers.

A rancher, Curlis Longlanais, whose farm had not been too badly damaged let the rescuers bunk down at his place. He had a huge recreation room complete with beds and showers, and this became the weekend home for the volunteers for months. Sonny Moss became the official cook for the volunteers.

Debra's work brought some wonderful rewards for her in the comments she heard from the ranch owners. The feed and hay that she brought, she was told, "made the difference between having to completely shut down, to sell out and give up their lifestyle" and being able to "hold on." The horses couldn't tell her in words but just watching them eat was reward enough. Numerous people and organizations nominated her for Animal Planet's "Animal Hero of the Year" award.

Leading all the convoys, Debra spent an enormous amount of her time, worked to exhaustion in horrific conditions, and went through two sets of tires on her truck. Would she do it again? "In a heartbeat."

For more information on Hopeful Haven check their website:
www.hopefulhaven.com

⤙ Saving Aragon

They say it takes a village to raise a child. Sometimes it takes a village to save a horse.

Susan Wirth and Juergen Frank were first time horse owners. With trainer Corinna Scheller's assistance, they had selected and imported a young chestnut gelding from Germany. He was, they hoped, their future dressage star.

Aragon settled in nicely at Lost Island Farm in Falls Village, Connecticut, where Susan trained with Corinna. He became a member of the family in no time, wooing everyone with his sweet temperament and enthusiasm for life. His beauty didn't hurt either: the rich chestnut coat and white markings were spectacular.

As winter set in, Susan and Aragon settled into a routine of dressage lessons, planning a future in the show ring.

That all changed the night of January 22, 2005. Susan and Juergen got an urgent phone call. Aragon was choking on some pellets. The new horse owners rushed through a blizzard to get to the barn.

By the time they got there, the vet on call from Millbrook Equine had Aragon comfortable and in good shape. Flush with the victory of having survived their first horse emergency, Susan and Juergen returned home.

It was but a brief reprieve. Twenty four hours later the news was far worse. Aragon had developed pleuropneumonia (involving not only the lungs, but the pleural space surrounding them), caused by food and bacteria that had fouled his lungs during the choking episode. He was feverish and his temperature soared. He was put on antibiotics immediately, and at first seemed to respond well. But then his temperature increased to dangerous levels. On February 9th he was shipped to Tufts University Large Animal Hospital in North Grafton, Massachusetts.

Juergen had gotten involved with horses primarily to spend time with his girlfriend. Tired of being left behind on weekends, he had started taking lessons and joined her at the barn. Now he and Susan owned Aragon together and the horse had become a family member. As Juergen says, "We didn't adopt him. He adopted us."

Of course, this was not what Juergen, or Susan, had envisioned. It was painful to watch their beautiful horse suffer. But they thought it would be short lived. Either he would get better quickly, or he would have to be put down.

It didn't play out either way. Instead, it evolved 48 hours at a time. The vets would tell them, "The next 48 hours is critical." Aragon would survive that 48 hours; Susan and Juergen would survive the enormous stress. And then it would happen all over again.

So they took it step by step. Financially, the step was huge. Bills at Tufts mounted quickly. But this horse, despite being critically ill, refused to surrender. It was Aragon's attitude, his will to survive, that enabled them to go on.

When the drugs Aragon was on were unable to resolve the problem, he had to undergo surgery. A thorocotomy, in which a portion of rib was removed so the surgeon could physically reach inside and remove septic fluid and infectious debris, was performed. He was too weak at this point for full anesthesia; he was partially sedated and was operated on while standing up.

Corinna, meanwhile, was right by Aragon's side every step of the way. She literally put her life on hold to help the horse recover, giving up lessons, and time with her fiancé. Susan and Juergen stayed with Aragon when they could and commuted back and forth from work to Tufts in order to pay the bills. In the two months Aragon ended up spending there, they put 12,000 miles on their car.

Aragon's friends from the barn came, too. They would just come and sit with him in his stall. Aragon wouldn't eat if his people weren't with him, so they made sure there was always someone he knew from Lost Island by his side.

The horse was so ill and so weakened, that no one was allowed near him without sterile gowns, gloves and masks. Tubes emerged from every part of his body—in fact he set a record at Tufts for the horse with the most tubes ever in his body.

The vets at Tufts were tremendously kind and compassionate, and all were quickly drawn into Aragon's circle of friends. As Susan says, he "bulldozed his way into everyone's heart." Students, vets, techs, all came to visit, and brought him his favorite strawberry flavored lifesavers. Everyone who met him wanted to help him. A massage therapist whose horse was also at Tufts gave Aragon massages, prompting some jealousy in Juergen!

The horse took comfort from his friends' presence; his friends took comfort from his fighting spirit. Dr. Daniela Bedenice, one of Aragon's vets at Tufts, said "His will to live was always there."

Despite constantly being subjected to tubes protruding from his body, people poking, prodding and stabbing, and confinement, Aragon never complained. He "never put his ears back, he always looked optimistic."

However, when Aragon felt particularly bad, he would stop eating. Fresh grass was recommended to entice him. Where do you find fresh grass in the middle of a New England winter?

You grow it, of course. Sue Boults, one of Corinna's students at Lost Island Farm, works at Geer Nursing Home in Canaan, Connecticut. Aragon's plight inspired residents to grow trays of Kentucky Blue Grass in their rooms.

Aragon loved it, eating the grass with relish. More residents took up the call, and Aragon soon had a good supply of fresh grass.

Susan's sister, who lives in New York City, bought up wheat grass sold at the Union Square Organic Market to take to Aragon. When her large buys prompted questions, a photo of Aragon was soon placed in his honor at the market.

Dr. Bedenice was amazed. "It was a phenomenal commitment by so many people" to save Aragon.

The administration at Tufts pitched in, listing Aragon as a special case that could advance veterinary learning. As a result, some of the vet services were performed free of charge.

Still, the vet bills were so high that Aragon came home sooner from the clinic than the vets would have liked. Arriving back at Lost Island on March 28, he still needed intensive care. Tubes and catheters sprouted from his body. He needed antibiotics, and medications to protect him from the side effects of antibiotics. He had life threatening blood clots in his right aorta and heart. Even treating him was dangerous. One of his medications was chloramphenicol, which is highly toxic to humans.

Asked if they ever thought of giving up, Susan and Juergen replied, "He never looked like he was giving up so there was never a question to stop." His welcoming nickers, lively eyes and greed for carrots told them this horse wanted to live.

Aragon wasn't home long when he developed another fever, and an ultrasound indicated more fluid in his lungs. Back to Tufts he went for another week. At this point, Susan jokes, "we would have sold our grandmother" to pay for his care. Again, he came home early, this time with a tube in his chest.

Home care was far more intensive than anyone had imagined. Corinna, even with all her experience, felt overwhelmed. They couldn't do it alone. It took the whole barn, and beyond, to make it work.

Yet the horse, Corinna says, "brought out the best in everyone."

Susan and Juergen would have to leave for work during the week and Corinna would take over. The round the clock vigils exhausted her to the point where she didn't think she could go on. A look at Aragon would revive her. If he was willing to fight, his human family was willing to fight with him!

So the boarders tag teamed, taking turns to care for the horse. Everyone just pulled together and said "We're going to make this happen." This outpouring of support from the boarders encouraged Susan, Juergen and Corinna during the worst of times.

Corinna gives tremendous credit to Millbrook Equine's Dr. Michelle Ferraro. Dr. Ferraro never gave up on Aragon; she always believed he would pull through even when other vets felt his case was hopeless. Dr. Ferraro made them believe that this was a battle they could win.

Although Corinna and her fiancé Les Fleming put their wedding plans on hold throughout Aragon's ordeal, their relationship was never threatened. Instead, it became stronger. Les never complained. Although he had no previous experience with horses, he would spend half the night convincing Aragon to eat. When Corinna felt she couldn't continue, Les would say "You can't give up now!"

She didn't. No one did. From his owners and friends to his vets, and all the people Aragon inspired along his path, everyone pulled for this amazing horse, and together, brought him through.

As he made progress, every milestone—the first turnout, the first walk under tack, the first trot under tack— "was a celebration." A party was held in Aragon's honor, and to thank all his friends who had seen him through. Among the guests were residents of Geer: a double amputee in a wheelchair, Francis Oaks (Aragon ate baby carrots off of his lap) and Olga Broggi, an octogenarian. Dr. Benedice made the trek from Tufts to attend.

As Susan began riding her horse again she took it slowly and carefully. This year, she was able to not only ride, but show, her horse. Although Susan was new to dressage and had never been to a show, they "won everything." Competing at Training Level, Aragon was high point winner in his first show with Jennifer Bacon, and reserve high point with Susan aboard. He was "right there for me" Susan says.

Watching Susan and Aragon turn down the centerline in their first class, Corinna couldn't help herself. "I was bawling," she says. She wasn't the only one in tears.

In show after show, class after class, from Kasson Ridge to Ox Ridge to HITS, Aragon won. So many people had helped him get better, and he wasn't about to let anyone down. He came through for everyone. Because of all the people who stuck with him, Aragon has a big future in front of him. He has inspired so many people, living proof that with a little help from your friends, you can go through hell and emerge on top.

⤳ Just Above A Whisper

Growing up on a dairy farm does have its advantages for horse crazy kids. You can always ride the cows—when your father isn't looking.

All of the kids in his family, says Mark Gomez, were "frustrated cowboys."

At 11, Mark's dad finally got him a pony. The poor pony worked "dawn to dusk. He was the neighborhood pony." Then Gomez got his first horse, a palomino mare which, although they didn't know it at the time, was in foal. The foal was the first horse Gomez ever trained. As he says, "it came out pretty well, it never killed me."

Gomez was interested in learning how to work with his horse, so he started reading about training techniques. He found an old correspondence course on horse training written by a Professor Barry from the turn of the century. There were a lot of horses in the early 1900s that performed tricks, like "counting." At a circus, there was often some horse trainer who could take a surly, "untrainable" horse into his tent, and come out a few hours later with a rideable horse. Some of it, Gomez says, was "smoke and mirrors" but some of it also was a good example of just what you could accomplish with a horse when you communicate properly with them.

From there he progressed to such well known natural horsemen as Ray Hunt, and Tom and Bill Dorrance. He also experimented a lot, using trial and error. What Gomez discovered is that there is a way to communicate with horses that involves not trying to dominate them.

Growing up, Gomez mainly rode bareback or western. It wasn't until later, when he became fascinated by polo, that he started riding English. The horses that became his polo ponies were runaways, or throwaways, horses no one wanted because they were considered uncontrollable. As he worked with them Gomez also turned to John Lyons for further education. Gomez believes we should educate ourselves about different disciplines because you can learn from everybody. "If you don't have an open mind, you're only cheating yourself," he says.

Gomez now considers natural horsemanship "basic foundation training for every discipline." It is, he says, about consistency, repetition, and communication. If you do something repeatedly the horse learns the system. One simple example of this is that most of us give our horses treats after we ride them. So the horse looks for the treat. If it is not forthcoming, the horse will nudge the rider for it. They have learned by repetition to expect the treat.

Horses do live by a hierarchy and need to know where they stand. If we don't take the leadership role they will and their ideas may not be the safest for us.

Gomez doesn't rush his training; he likes to take it slow. Watching him train horses, he says, is "like watching paint dry." Initially, horses are just "reacting to what we have presented to them." He presents the horses with a systematic approach and they react with consistent results.

Clients sometimes get frustrated: they want instant results.

But in the end, the client is really the trainer. Every interaction they have with their horse either reinforces good or bad behavior. As long as they are clear and consistent, horses will give you what you are asking for. Horses, says Gomez, "will bend over backwards to give us the right answer. We're really lucky about that!"

A major problem that arises is most people aren't consistent. The horse is trying hard to give the rider what they want, but can't figure it out because of the inconsistency, and as a result the horse gets frustrated. This is where problems can occur.

If the horse is not focused on us and we ask he's not going to hear us and not going to give us what we want. First we have to be focused, have a clear objective and present it logically so the horse can respond, rather than just react.

Gomez doesn't believe there are any horses past help, unless there's a physical problem that can't be remedied. He can't "train a horse out of a physical impairment." It's so important to always be listening, keeping the lines of communication open, because there may be another reason (like a physical problem) that the horse doesn't give you what you are asking for.

Gomez rides every horse with a snaffle and believes each horse should be capable of being ridden with a halter and lead rope. He says, "It's not what is on their head, it's what's in their brain."

One quite common problem that Gomez is asked for help with is a horse that gets into his owner's space. Gomez deals with this by raising his hands to block the horse until the horse turns its head away, in effect communicating "get out of my space." He rewards the slightest little change the horse makes. As soon as it starts to turn away, he drops his hands and pets the horse.

Then he backs away from the horse, and then comes back again. In his head he is thinking "out of my space" and he hunches over a bit, taking a "predator stance." As we are predators, horses are very wary of this predatory stance, and will back off. Sometimes Gomez will have to be a little bit more dramatic to get a reaction, crouching lower or waving his hands, or, in some cases, touching the horse to get it to back off. He uses as much pressure as the individual horse requires.

Again, as soon as the horse backs off, he rewards it, ceasing the "predatory" behavior and giving the horse a rub.

Of course, the next step is to teach the horse to come to you, as you don't want it to learn to always stay away! But it's important to only work on one thing at a time, before moving on to the next thing.

One of the horses that Gomez worked with that stands out in his mind was a big warmblood, a "brute" of a horse. He wasn't that tall but he was massive. And he had learned that he could dominate humans. It took two to three people to hold him while his rider mounted. His trainer felt that he was dangerous and wasn't comfortable working with him anymore but his owners loved him and wanted to see what could be done. Gomez went to evaluate him.

Arriving at the paddock, Gomez could immediately feel that this horse thought he was a play toy, that he could easily pick up a human and fling him through the air. He had little respect for people and was very aggressive when challenged. Despite that, he did have a big, kind eye.

The owners had only had him for four months and had treated him for an ulcer. They had hoped it would end his crankiness but it hadn't done the trick.

Gomez felt that this probably wasn't the right situation. The horse was definitely calling the shots, sure that he was the boss. Even if Mark worked with him, once he came back he felt the situation would deteriorate again. But the owners really wanted to give the horse a chance, so Gomez took him home.

The horse made great progress very quickly. Gomez as always was happy to have his round pen. It's great, he says, because you and the horse are not attached to each other. You can get away and the horse can get away.

The horse stayed a month and improved so much that soon Gomez' seven year old son was riding him. When he went back, the mother of the rider was very pleased and said the horse was much better. However, the trainer and owners agreed that embarking on a hectic show schedule this soon would not be in everyone's best interest. But this "unmanageable" horse turned into a nice horse, with a huge "before and after" difference. It was a great example of what consistency and correct communication can accomplish.

Gomez has tremendous respect for upper level dressage horses. He thinks it is "amazing the physical development that takes place as these horses progress up the levels."

He is also extremely impressed by Stacy Westfall, who with the Quarter Horse mare Whizards Baby Doll, competes in Freestyle Reining events with no saddle or bridle! (She is "some rider!" says Gomez) Watching an event like that should inspire all of us. Just what are our own horses capable of?!

These are examples of just what we can do with our horses, of what they are capable of, given the chance. If we present something correctly to a horse, it is, says Gomez, "limitless what we can do."

Horses Helping Humans (and Horses)

⤳ A Reason to Get up in the Morning

Exceller Farm in Poughquag, New York, rescues Thoroughbred racehorses and trains them for new careers. Some go on to become show horses, event horses or pleasure and trail horses. When Play After Dark came to the facility he presented a challenge for them. They weren't quite sure how to place him.

He was a sharp looking chestnut gelding, and had an incredible personality. But, thanks to life on the track, he also had ankles the size of oranges.

Michele Oren runs Exceller Farm, which is a Thoroughbred Retirement Foundation facility. She had recently gotten involved with therapeutic riding programs. Contacting a local chapter in Patterson, New York, she asked if they might be interested in "Play."

They were. And, it turned out, so was a young man who attended the facility.

Drew had Cerebral Palsy, which handicapped him in many ways. But when he met Play, it was love at first sight. "Play" was *his* to love and care for, as far as he was concerned. Drew groomed him, cleaned his stall and fed and watered him. With Play, Drew felt as though he was for once free of the handicap that was always present in his young life.

Play never judged him or told him what to do; he simply accepted him for who he was. Drew loved his new found sense of connection, freedom and responsibility.

Drew had always wanted to be a farmer. His mother got him two work shirts with *Farmer Drew* embroidered above the pocket for when he worked at Cascade Farm in Patterson, where Play lived.

This made his day; he was now an official farmer.

Drew knew Play inside and out. He enjoyed telling everyone how to behave around the horse and what words he responded to. "If I want him to go forward, I have to say 'walk on,' and 'whoa' to make him stop." Drew's relationship with Play gave him something that no other experience to date had provided: a sense of being a part of life, of being a regular kid.

On Play's sturdy back, Drew was master of all he surveyed and friends with a powerful and majestic animal. Play put purpose and meaning back into the young man's life. He *was* somebody.

One day Michele got a message from Margaret, Drew's mother. "You will not believe what this horse has done for my son Drew. He has been given a new life because of him. He looks so forward to going to the farm every day. On rainy days he cannot understand why he can't take care of him. He feels even though it is bad weather out, the horse needs his care and attention. As far as he is concerned, Play is his. His attitude and health have been much better since Play has come into his life. You have given him a reason to wake up each day."

Drew said that he loved animals "with all my heart, much the way I love my family. No demands. No conditions. No expectations. Just love them."

But there came the winter day when Michele got this message from Margaret: "I don't know how to tell you this but Drew is no longer with us. He has passed away. Play gave Drew the best gift he could have ever gotten. He gave him a reason to live and the strength to be more positive in his life. Play depended on him for love and care and Drew knew that. We can never thank you enough for the happiness that Play brought to our son over these past couple of years."

Everyone misses Drew, but no one misses him more than Play.

(Our thanks to Michele Oren for this story.)
If you are interested in adopting an ex-racehorse, or would like to find out what you can do to help, contact www.trfinc.org

⤳ Progress

They were working Clydesdales, draft horses whose names all began with the same letter. Huge though they were, they were named after delicate flowers. Home was in upstate Vermont, infamous for its long cold winters. Infamous also for its spring, known better as mud season.

The old farmer loved his Clydesdales. He was teased sometimes, teased because people felt that the horses were outmoded, that tractors and other motorized vehicles had rendered them dinosaurs. But he ignored them. His horses worked. They pulled the manure spreader, they pulled hay wagons. They earned their keep.

Besides, tractors don't nicker when you open the barn doors in the morning.

One spring, mud season was particularly bad. The deep mud sucked off people's shoes, coated their clothes. Cars lay stranded in the ruts of dirt roads turned to quagmire. People chose their routes home carefully in order to not lose their cars en route.

The utility company was attempting to lay cable, but they were having problems. Their trucks were getting stuck. They couldn't maneuver in the deep, sucking mud. The big wooden spools wound with cable were sitting in mud, too. Well, perhaps not sitting so much as sinking.

The old man was amused at the call for help. So, the new, modern equipment couldn't handle what Vermont could dish out?

And so, his horses came. The farmer brought his huge bays with their white feathered legs to see what could be done. But he didn't just look at the situation and shake his head, as the utility men had done.   He hitched his team to the tractors, the rolls of cables, and whatever piece of equipment had become ensnared by the thick goop.   And they pulled out the machinery.   Their huge, dinner plate size feet dug into the mud and gave them traction, while their powerful bodies provided the energy to do what no manmade vehicle could.

And when the vehicles were all freed, the horses, those outmoded throwbacks to a former era, laid the cable.

⟶ KING JODY

He has a knack for showing up in people's, and horse's lives when they need him. His loyalty, patience and kindness make him the kind of horse that no one ever forgets.

Before she could even talk, Nancy knew she wanted a horse. Her mom put it in her baby book: all her daughter could think about was horses. Her parents couldn't tear her away from them. When they went to the Bronx Zoo, Nancy headed straight for the area featuring farm animals, right to the horses, and never wanted to leave.

Every year, she put a horse on her Christmas and birthday lists. It was usually the only item on her list. The horse never came.

She tried winning the Arabian that was given away yearly at the National Horse Show at Madison Square Garden. She never won.

As an adult, she still hadn't achieved her dream of a horse of her own. Now she was a single mother, working full time and going to school, and the idea seemed out of the question.

Her friend Gus, however, had other ideas. He thought now was the perfect time. With all that hard work and stress in her life, Nancy *needed* a horse. So he dragged her with him to every stable on Long Island, putting her up on every horse that he could find that was for sale. Unfortunately, most of them were way out of her price range.

Gus had two horses of his own: Comanche Adam, a big Cavalry Morgan and an Arabian mare named A Rose A Gem. Gus had purchased Rosie out of a pasture where she was playing lawn ornament as a result of being too much for her owner. He thought she would be a good endurance partner. She was. In fact they placed fourth in all around standings in the middle weight division that they competed in.

One day Gus took Comanche on a trail ride with his friend Laura. Laura had also wanted a horse her whole life and had never had one. But when she got cancer and had the good fortune to go into remission, she knew it was time. She went out and bought herself a horse, King Jody.

King Jody is a 15 hand bay Quarter Horse who greatly resembles his famous great granddaddy, King 234. He was the first (and only) horse Laura looked at. It was an instant connection. Laura put down the $1000 and took her new horse home.

King is a gentleman, the kind of horse a child can stand under. In fact, he became so popular with the children that when Laura rode him to the park, neighborhood kids would run back in their houses to grab carrots to feed to King. It could take Laura a *long* time to get to the park.

Laura's instinct had been right on the money. King was the perfect horse for her. He had been trained as a cutting horse and was so good at it that all you needed to do was point to a cow and get out of his way. But it was as a steady trail horse that he really shined for Laura.

Unfortunately, Laura had come out of remission and was now receiving a second round of treatment for non-Hodgkin's Lymphoma. She needed someone to help share her expenses on King. Gus put two and two together and suggested that Nancy give Laura a call.

She did. She met Laura, and she met King and instantly the three of them bonded. Nancy began riding and sharing responsibility for King, and living her dream. King meanwhile took care of Laura, being wonderful and steady as always when she was weak from treatment, or providing her the welcome relief she needed from the stress of the disease. She would often insist on going straight from treatment to the barn to hug her four legged friend.

King's sixth sense let him know when Laura needed special care.

Nancy and King lost Laura when she lost her fight with cancer. Although Nancy had promised Laura that she would take care of King she also told her that King would always be *Laura's* horse.

Nancy and King dabble in cattle penning and western pleasure, but mostly enjoy the peaceful woods and streams of Manorville, New York. King has proven himself to be just what Nancy wanted: a perfect partner. And a great trail guide. When Nancy gets lost, King is the one who finds the path back home.

Raised in the south as he was, King is ever the gentleman. He will let Nancy know just what he thinks about something, but he's sure to be polite about it. He's also quite the ladies man, and when there are mares about, King will arch his neck and strut his stuff.

Once a year, Laura's niece and nephew come to ride King. King is ever solicitous of the kids. Where are they? He turns his head to check on their location, so careful not to get them in harm's way. Nancy never fails to be impressed at his keen sense of safety and responsibility.

And it's not only his human friends that King takes care of.

King and Gus' horse Rosie were best pasture buddies. One evening, there was a violent thunder storm. In the morning Nancy and Gus found the two horses standing flank to flank. Rosie had badly fractured her pastern. The vet advised that she be put down. That same morning, Gus received his certificate and jacket for his and Rosie's fourth place overall standing in endurance riding.

Rosie's only hope was through the services of Dr. Reed, an orthopedic specialist at Belmont Race Track. Gus had to give Rosie a chance, to try to save her, even though there was no guarantee of recovery and it would require a lengthy lay-up. He drove to the track and waited in the pitch black of early morning, x-rays on the seat beside him. When Dr. Reed arrived, he approached him with x-rays in hand, explaining that Rosie was an endurance horse who had fractured her pastern. Dr. Reed looked at the xrays right there in the parking lot, by the light of day.

"Bring her in tomorrow morning and we'll operate" he said. Gus brought her in. The operation went well.

When Rosie came home after the operation, she was confined to her stall with a cast and screws in her leg. Her recovery depended a great deal upon her ability to remain calm and quiet.

It was King who took it upon himself to supervise her recovery. Occupying a run-in next to Rosie's stall, he had free access to the attached paddock. Between the two horses' stalls there was a small window. King remained there day after day, week after week, in his stall with his eye to the window, supervising Rosie's return to health.

It was his steadiness, his unwavering support, that enabled the high strung Rosie to remain quiet and recuperate. His uncanny sixth sense once again came to light. He knew just when it was OK for him to leave the stall, and just how far he could go without upsetting Rosie. For months, he continued his vigil. And Rosie recovered.

King was the horse Laura always dreamed of, the horse Nancy wanted all her life and a best friend to Rosie. He came to each of them just when they needed him. The polite southern gentleman has been, and continues to be, a gift in many lives.

⤳ Long Time Coming

He was angry, violent, looking for a fight. Considered a juvenile delinquent by most who knew him, he was in and out of rehab, in and out of trouble. The boy had been physically abused by his father, who then abandoned the family. His mother, a victim of abuse herself, found she just could not handle him.

He ended up in a stepfamily, where he turned to drugs, particularly crystal meth. Most people who tried to get near him, to help, found that he was impossible to love. As hard as they might try, no one could see the good in him.

No one, that is, except LT.

LT is Dr. Lisa Guerin's therapy horse. Lisa's program, Instinctual Recovery ™, which is based near Los Angeles, helps clients work past the abuse and violence they have suffered in their lives. Lisa specializes in trauma and addiction. She has discovered that Equine Assisted Therapy is particularly effective because people will take feedback without defenses from a horse. They know the horse isn't judging them and doesn't have an agenda.

LT is known throughout the country: people fly in from as far away as New York to work with him. He is so effective that sometimes just one session with him in the roundpen can cut through six months to a year of therapy in Lisa's office. He is, says Lisa, "always amazing and right on." The pride she feels in her horse shines through in her voice.

In the Instinctual Recovery ™ Program, Lisa, LT and clients work together in a roundpen. Sometimes Lisa works with a client privately, but quite often she runs a group and one at a time will come into the ring while the others in the group witness. She asks each client to think of an intention of what they'd like to work on or get out of the experience. During the conversation, LT is free to interact (or not), resonate and express whatever runs through him, and that often mirrors what is happening with clients as they discuss their lives with Lisa.

LT grew up in an abusive situation himself, starting life with a troubled alcoholic who beat him before eventually committing suicide. His next home was at a ranch, where his job was to take customers on trail rides. He shared this home with about 40 other horses. His owner did the best she could, but was hard put to support and care for her ever growing collection of horses. The food was of poor quality and the care was rudimentary.

It was here that Lisa and LT became acquainted. Lisa was "auditioning" for a therapy horse. She met the 11 year old National Show Horse (half Arabian/half Saddlebred) after turning down nearly 30 horses before him. She knew instantly that he had the sensitivity for the job.

But it took her five years to wrestle him free from his life at the ranch and have him finally become her own horse. Ironically, when she got his papers, his full name turned out to be "Long Time Coming." Lisa knows this was no accident: it is so appropriate not only for the experience she had obtaining LT, but for a therapy horse who works a lot with helping addicts and trauma survivors come into their recovery and healing.

Since recruiting him, LT has become an essential part of her program. The sensitive horse is "very confident in his mastery of what he's doing." His own life of abuse, Lisa feels, has probably endowed him with the extra sensitivity he needs to understand and help others. Lisa says she probably will never work with another horse who is so invested in the healing of the Human Spirit as LT.

Lisa is of course well versed in the ways LT relates to people, the things he does to help people work through their issues and leave them behind. Yet she says he "can still find new and creative and spontaneous ways to communicate that are uncanny and brilliant." One day, he proved that to her yet again. He did something different, something she had never seen him do before—and has never done again.

It was the last day of their tenure at the barn in Malibu where Lisa had run her program for five years. They were about to move to new quarters, to their own place, LionHeart Ranch Equestrian and Healing Arts Center. The name was chosen to honor all those who have the courage of heart--lionheartedness--to heal.

It was the last group of the day.

The "juvenile delinquent" who was so blocked, so angry, had been sent to them. It wasn't his first rehab. People who had worked with him before were shaking their heads. He was very difficult and manipulative, and constantly wanted to "butt up against authority" they told Lisa.

She saved him for last so that he could witness the interaction between other members of the group and LT. He was a big dude, built like a solid block, with a big chest. Lisa was bracing herself for a fight, ready to go into alpha mode, ready to take the same posture that everyone else had taken with the boy.

But when they went into the ring, LT stalemated the incipient fight. LT can be tough with clients when he needs to be. But today he knew that wasn't the right approach. Quite the opposite. They walked once around the ring, with LT on a lead rope. Then they stopped. LT stood perfectly still. Lisa noted that the boy's typical belligerent attitude had not surfaced. Instead he was very honest and soft. He began to share, letting himself be a bit vulnerable.

LT was very still, projecting "it's just me and you and we're not going anywhere." He knew he needed to bond with the boy, and he knew just how he was going to do it. He took a long, deep breath.

Then he lay down right at the boy's feet. This was a prey animal exposing himself to a predator, to a boy who lived his life in a predatory fashion. LT lay completely at his mercy, exposing himself.

The boy was surprised. "Oh shit, what's happening?" The group was equally stunned.

Lisa calmed him, telling him it was OK, and suggesting he sit down as well. He did. LT put his head into the boy's lap. He went into a state of reverence, a pure, sweet state. Peace emanated from the boy as well. It was utter connection, the essence of this horse to the essence of the young man.

For twenty minutes, there was silence. The boy stroked LT's head, the two of them sharing the peace and connection. The group watched in awe.

Lisa was, as she has so often been, amazed at her horse's superior knowing, of his access to something much bigger than all of them. She said to the boy, "You must be very safe for this horse to do that, to make himself so vulnerable."

LT had seen in this young man what no one else had seen. And he felt it: he felt his own worth and saw a side of himself that no one before LT had known was there.

LT's message to the world was "You are all wrong. I'm going to give my entire being to this person so that he can see who he truly is. I see this kernel in this person that no one else has seen."

Lisa explained to her client just how special this was, that it was something LT had never done before and that it proved how worthy the young man was, how he was a part of, not apart from, humanity.

The young man clearly received the message LT had given to him. He accepted his worth, opened up and was able to make different choices in his life. He was no longer in a fight for survival. He was safe.

The wisdom that LT displayed was out of the realm of everyone's thinking. He was, once again, right on. As Lisa said, "he was a genius at knowing where the healing was, to prostrate himself in front of someone who was so closed off and so aggressive." He completely gave himself to this young man, and in so doing, opened a window, opened a soul, that no one knew was there.

⟶⦂ TRISTAN

Our first horse always holds a special place in our hearts. For Elaine Lang, that horse was Tristan.

Tristan was a Christmas present from her husband, a 15 hand seal brown Morgan/Quarter Horse cross. Although Tristan had been gelded, he was gelded late, retaining some of his stallion traits. One of those was his desire to protect his herd, in this case, his band of three mares and Elaine.

Tristan was a tough little horse. Sometimes he and Elaine would be out all day, riding the trails around the barn in Brookfield, Connecticut, where he was kept. Sometimes too, Garrett, Elaine's son, would accompany them, perched behind the saddle.

In the winter, Tristan wore sleigh bells around his neck. He liked the sound: his ears would flick back and forth in order to catch the jingling.

Near the trails and parallel to them ran a railroad track. It was something that always concerned Elaine. She would watch for the train, worried about how Tris might react. What if he spooked towards the train? In order to not take chances, Elaine always timed their rides so they would be back at the barn before dark.

But one day Elaine misjudged and it was dusk as they made their way down the train tracks towards home. As dusk turned to evening, she suddenly saw the track lights go on. A train was coming! Both sides of the track were impassible swamp and there wasn't enough time to ride back to solid ground. It was dark, with no moonlight, impossible for Elaine to find the trail that ran parallel to the tracks now.

Tristan kept trying to go to the left, but Elaine would frantically pull him back to the right. Terrified, she galloped him back and forth in a panic searching for the trail. But there was no finding it in the blackness.

In the midst of her fright, a flashback suddenly came to her. She went back to a late summer day years ago when she and a friend were exploring new trails.

They had come to the edge of a lake. Looking down, Elaine had found she could see through the water clear to the bottom. She asked Tristan to step into the lake, and was surprised when he balked. He had never refused to go forward when asked. Again she asked, and again he refused. Then she had insisted, slapping him with her crop. Tristan walked into the water and immediately sank up to his tail in quicksand like mud. Elaine's girlfriend, who had stayed on the road, screamed as she watched her friend and Tristan sink into the lake.

Elaine hadn't known what to do. If she'd jumped down she would have sunk up to her waist. But how was her small horse to manage the weight of rider and tack in such deep mud?

Before she'd been able to react, Tristan had given two huge Herculean leaps, pulling them out of the mud and up onto the road. Scrambling off of him, Elaine had checked every inch of her horse, thinking he must have wrenched muscles. All the while she'd thanked him and asked his forgiveness for her stupidity. She promised she would never doubt his instincts again.

The flashback ended and she snapped back to the present. Dropping the reins, she released all control to Tristan and yelled for him to take them home. He quickly swung left, the direction he had been trying to take all along, galloped about 300 feet down the track and plunged in the total darkness into the woods.

Elaine lay flat on his neck, her arms over her head, trying not to get knocked off by branches she couldn't see. Minutes later, they were on the road. They were safe!

It wasn't the last time Tristan got her out of a jam, but it was the last time Elaine ever ignored his wisdom.

Although Tristan has been gone now for a long time, every winter Elaine hangs his sleigh bells on her mailbox, nestled amongst the bows and evergreen, and remembers her special horse.

OVERSEAS

⟶ AN IRISH ADVENTURE

The two sisters, Jennifer and Christa, were coming up on land-mark birthdays: 30 and 35 respectively. There was no question about it: something special was needed to mark the occasion.

A trip to Ireland—a foxhunting trip—was planned.

As a young girl, Jennifer had visions of sailing over jumps with her own horse. She did get a horse, or rather, a pony, but by the time Jennifer was ready to jump, her pony had become too old for it. So the dream was put on hold.

This trip was a big one for Jennifer. For the first time in her life she needed a passport to get where she was going.

Once the sisters decided on their destination, anticipation set in. They made plans, and they made reservations. Time couldn't move fast enough until their departure, for this, the trip of a lifetime.

And finally the day arrived. As they took off, Jennifer was filled with an overwhelming sense of adventure. Early in the morning, they arrived in Ireland. Looking around her, Jennifer was immediately smitten by the breathtakingly beautiful landscape.

The sisters brought Ruth Cook, their 82 year old grandmother along, wanting her to be part of their big adventure. She loved the plane ride: hey little bottles of free Bailey's Irish Cream—life is sweet!

Although Christa was an experienced foxhunter, (in fact she had helped create a hunt in Vermont where she lives), Jennifer was new to the sport. At home she had ridden in some hunter paces to give her a bit of practice, but they were really not comparable to the real thing.

And Jennifer and Christa were not just hunting but hunting in Ireland, of all places! Everyone had heard tales of the huge fences and crazy Irishmen.

Willie Leahy of the famous Galway Blazers had been contracted to provide the horses. Willie has hundreds of horses at his farm, reliable and experienced hunters. Jennifer had specific requirements for him. She wanted a big horse, one who was athletic, yet was kind enough to show her the ropes. The reason she wanted a big horse was simple. This way the fences wouldn't look quite so high!

Willie's instructions to Jennifer and Christa were to meet him at the pub to pick up their horses. After all, this is Ireland. And there is a lot of justification for meeting at the pub. A little (or a lot) of fortification is needed before one tackles the walls and ditches of Irish farm land. Whisky and hot port are the order of the day.

As they drew near the pub, Jennifer saw long rows of tiny trailers (horse boxes or lorries) pulled by tiny cars lining the narrow lanes adjacent to the building. The whole concept was just a little nerve-wracking. Out of one of these lorries is pulled a strange horse, one you've never seen before, much less ridden. And now you're going to trust this horse to carry you at high speeds over mammoth walls and across fields strewn with rocks like minefields.

No wonder you meet at a pub!

For Jennifer, this trip was the start of a new chapter in her life. It wasn't just a test of her courage, but it was a psychological test as well. Jennifer liked life within the lines. Now she was going to have to let go, to abandon herself to a strange horse and unfamiliar people in a sport that was both fast and dangerous.

As Jennifer's horse was brought over to her, she noticed that "Red" was exactly what she had requested. He was over 17 hands high, with a nice long neck. Not only was he huge, but he proved to be an "absolute gentleman." And despite his size, he wasn't coarse. He had a good mane, important to Jennifer so she had something to hang on to. His saddle, she discovered, was really comfy, with big knee rolls, something she could feel secure in. "This is good!" she thought.

As they headed out for that first hunt, Jennifer felt such a feeling of freedom and independence. It was no longer just a dream, it was happening! As she came up an incline and saw the first wall, she knew there was no turning back now. She was on her way! She found a tiny spot to jump, and then, pure adrenaline set in. "You can't turn back; it's like the start of a roller coaster ride! Here we go! Your heart is in your throat, but you are utterly alive in anticipation of what is to come."

Fox hunting in Ireland is different than in the states, it is a part of their culture. It is a family tradition that has been handed down for hundreds of years, a national sport that families embrace from the youngest to the oldest. It's such a big part of Irish culture that, during hunting season, if the weather promises a good day for foxhunting, children are pulled out of school! From October to April, every Tuesday, Thursday and Saturday, the locals foxhunt.

The scenes that Jennifer took in were extraordinary. Children on their Connemara ponies were hunting right up at the top of the field, their grey ponies popping easily over the huge walls.

She noticed large stocky men, clad in wellies and carhartt type jackets and ancient hats, riding along with the hunters in their red coats and breeches. These, she learned, were the landowners of the fields they were hunting on. As a courtesy the hunt always brought a horse along for them to ride.

Jennifer found herself in a huge crowd of people. She found that often as many as 75 people and 50 hounds turned out for a day of foxhunting. Trotting down the middle of a street surrounded by all these people, Jennifer experienced a real sense of pride, of being part of something so integral to Irish life. The excitement was contagious, and there was a strong sense of camaraderie.

All of her senses were overcome: the sound of 75 sets of hooves clopping along the road, the sight and smells of the lush green of the Irish countryside, the feel of the well broken in tack and the big, solid horse she was sitting on. "Awesome," she thought, knowing that didn't even begin to cover it.

No one had overstated the size of the walls surrounding Irish fields. "Oh my God!" thought Jennifer, as she approached a mammoth fieldstone wall, "Should I be jumping this?" These walls, after all, were built to *retain* livestock, to keep them in! Why on earth were they on livestock, jumping them?

But she was at the end of the field. Seventy four other people, including little kids on ponies had already jumped it. Well, she thought, if they did it, so can I! Everyone else was so confident and carefree. Jennifer got swept up in the emotions and felt confident herself. The attitude of the Irish was: just go and have fun. And she did.

The experience was wild, exactly what Jennifer needed. Used to always being in control, now, there was little she could control. It was all about blind faith. Riders didn't know what they were getting into until they were in mid-air because they couldn't see beyond the massive walls they were jumping. After taking off Jennifer might spot a branch on the landing side, or rocks that horses before her had kicked loose. She would have to duck or swerve. The only thing she could do was look for the most reasonable place to jump that she could find and then trust Red.

Jennifer discovered that the Irish take on foxhunting was one of pure fun and absolute equality. It wasn't about who's got the best horse or who rides the best or has been doing it the longest.

At first Jennifer worried about her form, about how well she rode. But when she found herself trotting down a beautiful country road, worried about whether she was on the correct diagonal or not, she had an epiphany. "What am I doing?" she wondered, "No one cares, no one notices, just ride!" After that, she left her worries behind her.

The whole foxhunting scene is just "a beautiful photograph, everything is so lush. The red foxes, simple homes, beautiful horses and scarlet coats all against the green, green landscape." Some of the riders seemed to have stepped out of an art museum, exhibiting the old style hunt seat of legs forward, bodies tilted backwards.

The first hunt that Jennifer and Christa went on lasted for nearly six hours (which they discovered was quite typical.) Although they were having a fabulous time, there was one small problem. They were starving! And they hadn't thought to bring any food.

Luckily, some of the experienced hunters shared their survival technique: bring chocolate. A Cadbury Dairy Milk Bar to be specific. They did manage to find someone willing to part with just a crumb of their chocolate and it tasted like the sweetest meal on earth!

For the next hunt they were prepared. Each had their *own* Dairy Milk Bar!

As with all sports, there are tricks for success, and it didn't take long for the sisters to figure some of them out. Huge walls become smaller after an entire field has passed through—some horses knock stones off as they jump. So if you wait, the wall gets smaller and more jumpable! Certain people in the hunt are good to ride behind: others are not. You learn. People whose horses stop at the walls and ditches could become obstacles for you to crash into, so you avoid them. Others seems to have an uncanny knack for just the right spot in the wall to jump, so following a couple lengths behind them can make for a particularly fun and comfortable hunt.

The horses are so good at making their way through the melee that Jennifer swears they have radar on their feet. They know precisely where the stones have fallen and where they lie strewn across the fields, and avoid them with ease. They are, she says, "unbelievable athletes."

When the hunt was over, the field returned to the pub. There was no fussing over the horses. You loosen your horse's girth, wrap your reins around your horse's neck and up the horses go onto the trailer. "They load themselves," says Jennifer, they're such, "good, good animals."

Then it's back inside the pub—for more whiskey.

Jennifer changed a lot on her trip to Ireland. She learned to let go, to have faith and trust her horse. And she gained something else in Ireland. Her childhood vision of sailing over fences came true. In an unforgettable way.

⌇ VIENNA

"I was always in love with the horses."

It was the late 1930s, and the horses were the world famous Lippizans of Vienna, Austria.

She was 15 with bright red hair, and a disposition to match. She worked hard, attending school and then helping out at her father's store whenever school was not in session. There was no such thing as a Saturday off, no playtime for Vilma.

Wednesdays were her one escape. Every Wednesday, she would leave work, catch a trolley and travel across the graceful city to the Spanish Riding School. The horses were rehearsing, and the rehearsal was open to the public for free.

To a child, and to anyone watching, the experience was magical. Crystal chandeliers sparkled from the ceiling, relflecting off the silky white coats of the stallions. Riders dressed in cardinal red coats and polished black boots contrasted strikingly with the white walls, the white horses.

The elegant setting for the performance was the Winter Riding School in the Imperial Palace. The palace, commissioned by Emperor Karl VI, dated from 1735.

The incredible leaps and acrobatics of the horses, tracing back to movements once used in battle, was a four footed ballet. Vilma would sit, rivetted. Sometimes the horses performed in groups, dancing intricate patterns around the school. Some horses, those that were particularly talented, performed alone. Vilma never tired of watching the magnificent athletes.

After the performance, she would sneak around the back to the entrance to the stables. She saved lump sugar and brought it with her to feed the horses. Trying to gain admittance, she would be met by one of the riders.

"You're not allowed in here." he would tell her.

"I know," she would answer.

But always she got in. How could a soldier refuse the child? In her radiant eyes, he could see what a treat it was to come and visit the horses, to feed them sugar cubes.

The soldier would watch as Vilma told the horses stories, while she fed them her treats. Sometimes she made up stories, sometimes she would tell them about her life. She knew they were listening, understanding.

But Vienna was changing. Swastikas were appearing everywhere. Vilma's friends, her neighbors, crossed the streest when they saw her, refusing any contact. In the country of her birth, Vilma Kurzer became an undesirable person. She told the horses about it, about the pain of being abandoned by her own country. She told them of the fear, of how her parents would turn white whenever a knock came at the door. Then she said good bye to them and left, fleeing to America.

Soon, bombs were descending on Austria, on Vienna. The horses were endangered—by the bombs, by invading forces. With no respect for human life, the invaders certainly did not understand the power and beauty of the horses.

The horses were rescued, saved by Colonel Alois Podjasky and General George Patton (a horseman himself). Risking their own lives, they heroically evacuated the horses to St. Martin in upper Austria.

The Lipizzans continue to amaze and entertain crowds around the world.

And the red headed girl, now 94 years old, has never forgotten them.

Twister and Heather competing at the Southeastern
Reining Horse Association Spring Celebration in
Williamston, North Carolina

Photo: Team Extreme Media

Frolic and friends

Will Faudree on Antigua at Burghley, 2007

Photo: Equestrian Photographic Services

95

Impy and Camille

Carol and Mac

*Platinum Plus and Sharon Santandra splash through
a water complex.*

Courtesy of Connecticutphoto, Brian Wilcox

Aragon and his "family" at a horse show
at HITS, Saugerties, New York

Photo: Juergen Frank

LT

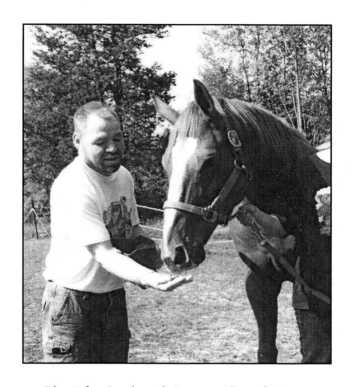

Play After Dark with Drew at Cascade Farm

John Benson Photo

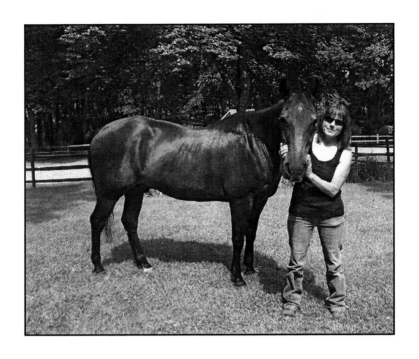

King and Nancy

Tristan

Lightnin Cat

Silly

Aly Ad Libs competes in a Grand Prix in Ocala, Florida, with Pat Garthwaite up.

Courtesy of O'Neill photos

*Ima Good 1-2 competing at Harrisburg, Pennsylvania
with Patty van Housen*

Randi Muster Photo

Bethesda After Dark (Shadow) and Scott Monroe on course.

Photo: Pics of You, John Robinson

Whizards Baby Doll and Stacy Westfall competing in
"Road to the Horse" held in Murfreesboro, Tennesee

Tanya Corzatt Photo

Josi

Love at First Sight

⤳ Lightnin Cat

He was bred to win the Triple Crown. With the highest con-
nections in racing: bred by Roger Young at Overbrook Farm, and
trained by the legendary D. Wayne Lukas, Lightnin Cat was born
to be a champion.

Five people attended the birth of this son of Storm Cat, the pre-
eminent sire of the day. Such breeding was nothing less than
equine royalty, and when Cat grew older and began his career, he
traveled with a coterie of attendants, in private planes.

In Lightnin Cat's first race, in California, he was cut off, bumped
and pushed back. He faced every problem any young racehorse
could encounter, and yet still came from behind to finish a strong
fourth. His championship breeding showed.

For his next race, Lightnin Cat was flown to Saratoga. His performance in California had proven he was worthy of competing at
this illustrious track. But here, too, he encountered bad luck.
Worse, this time, than the bumps and shoves he'd encountered in
California: this time the young horse was injured.

He was flown again, this time to Kentucky. Cat was brought to
the top equine surgeon in the country, Dr. Larry Bramlage at Rood
and Riddle Equine Hospital in Lexington.

The vet warned his client that Lightnin Cat could no longer race
at his former level. The horse's injury was serious enough that it
would not allow that kind of athletic performance.

The stallion returned to racing, to New York's Belmont Park.
Only now he ran in claiming races. Although he was still with
Lukas, he was no longer in the first string.

That didn't prevent him from winning. Cat won a $34,000 race at Saratoga. And in claiming races, he kept getting claimed. With his lineage, he always found a buyer.

Lightnin Cat's life had changed markedly from its initial promise. He went from barn to barn, every two or three months finding himself in a new home. His injury had weakened his ability, but even as he went to smaller tracks and smaller purses, he still kept "hitting the board," making money for his owners and trainers.

Track photos document the changes in Cat's life. Now four, the horse was no longer the proud spirit of his first races. Nor was it only he that changed. The tracks were rougher, even the grooms were very different. Lukas' grooms were attired in spiffy matching outfits. Grooms at these lower level tracks wore torn jeans and tee shirts.

In one claiming race, Cat found himself claimed by Steven Jerkens (son of Hall of Famer Allen Jerkens). Attracted by Cat's breeding, Jerkens decided to give him a try. The only problem was, Lightnin Cat could barely walk back to the barn.

He had shattered his knee, prompting the vet who xrayed him to say that the horse's knee looked as though a grenade had gone off in it.

Loraine Romeo happened to be at the track that day. Loraine runs a farm in Gardiner, New York, On Track Training Center, where she and her daughter Renee breed and train both race and show horses. Loraine has a reputation for being able to save horses that most people would give up on as doomed.

Lightnin Cat certainly qualified.

When Jerkens spotted her, he flagged her down. He told Loraine, "This horse is done. If I keep him, I'll only have to put him down. But if you want him, you can have him."

Lorraine took one look at him. Storm Cats are built. This horse was gorgeous, with a beautiful, sloping shoulder, wide hips and powerful hindquarters. She would take him all right, even if he *was* standing on three legs. So he had a "knee problem." She had fixed things before, she could fix this.

So Lightnin Cat, accustomed to traveling in luxury on planes, hobbled onto a horse trailer hauled by an old Ford pickup.

Lorraine creatively fashioned a cast for him, using heavy clay, paper towels, soft support bandages and, the universal fix-it: duct tape, "tons" of duct tape.

For a month, Cat was kept confined to a stall.

Then Loraine moved him to another facility, in Middletown, New York, which had a swimming pool. A stall she leased there had just opened up when another horse left. Swimming would be good for Cat, she thought.

The vet who worked at the facility, Dr. Joe Malone, spied the limping horse and asked Loraine what was up. He took xrays of Cat. "You can't be serious," he said. "What do you think you're doing?"

"He's a Storm Cat," answered Loraine, "We have to give him a shot."

Ignoring the vet's words, she instead trusted her gut feeling.

Cat took to swimming like a fish. He thrived on it. And although he limped to the pool, he always seemed a little sounder when he finished his swim. After two months of the therapy, one day he walked out sound.

Loraine called to the vet. "Look! He's sound!"

"Sound?" he asked. "That horse will never be sound! He'll always be useless!"

But he was astounded at what he saw. "That's amazing!" he said.

Cat came back to On Track, where he began walking, and then jogging. He was sound.

About that time, one of Loraine's students, Moira Roberts, needed a horse to ride. The horse she had been riding, which had never been a particularly good match, had been sold. There were two potentials for Moira—one was Cat. Loraine had a strong feeling that Moira would pick Cat, and she was right. Moira went to the stall, opened the door, and went, "WOW!!"

It was love at first sight.

Soon, Cat was doing flatwork, being reschooled for the show world. He never took a lame step, so Loraine decided it was time to start jumping him. Lightnin Cat wasn't sure what to do with his first jump. Crashing through it, he knocked rails in every direction.

Cat was confused. Fences were always something to keep him in. And now they wanted him to jump out of them?

Cat was being turned out with a buddy, a racetrack retiree named Diamond Anchor. Diamond had already been started over fences. Soon Cat started jumping the fences in the ring instead of crashing through them. Maybe, Loraine and Moira joke, Diamond Anchor explained to Cat that he was now supposed to jump the fences instead of stay inside them.

Whatever the reason, Cat grew to love jumping. His bloodlines showed: he was brave, never stopping at any fence, no matter how scary.

And although initially Loraine would worry about his knee, after a year without a problem, she never thought about it again.

Soon it was time for Cat to go to his first show. In his former incarnation as a racetrack star, he would be dressed for his journeys in fuzzy wraps and a halter encased in fuzzy fleeces. Now, to go to the show, Moira once more dressed him in fuzzies. And Cat remembered. Just as before, he was "the man." He felt like the horse he had been while he was with Lukas.

However, with Lukas, Cat was loaded onto planes. That, Cat felt, was how he should travel! What was it with these people wanting him to travel by trailers? Didn't they know better? Royalty doesn't take road trips.

Cat wanted nothing to do with this common mode of transportation. He would get on the trailer but he hated it once it started moving. Rolling across the ground was bumpy, not at all like the smooth rides he was used to with air travel. Finally Loraine solved the problem: she gave Cat a whole stall on her trailer. At least Cat could now move around and make himself more comfortable.

To avoid embarrassment, Loraine and Moira chose a small schooling show at Hillside Meadows in Connecticut for Cat's introduction to horse shows. They needn't have feared embarrassment. They had a star on their hands. Cat was champion.

It hadn't taken Moira long to fall in love with the handsome, cocky son of Storm Cat. She asked Loraine repeatedly to sell her the horse. But Lorraine said no, she wouldn't sell the big horse. Even Moira's husband tried to buy him for his wife. The answer was the same for him.

Then Moira's father died. She was devastated. She drowned her sorrows in Cat. She begged Loraine to sell her the horse. Loraine still refused to sell him.

But she did give him to Moira.

Cat has won championship after championship, zone awards and year end awards. The only limitation he has is that, at the biggest shows, Moira has to show him in equitation instead of the hunters. His formerly shattered knee can't quite bend to the extent of the other one so he is not perfectly even over the fences.

Cat loves his work, and if he gets too much time off, Moira says, he becomes "a bear." At shows he gets pumped. He knows this is his new job and he is going to go into that ring and show the judge and the crowd what a star looks like.

Cat was born to be a champion. It was in his genes. As Renee says, "like all Storm Cats, he was bred to be an athlete."

His breeders meant for him to be a champion on the racetrack. Fate intervened and his racing career was cut short. But it didn't prevent him from fulfilling his destiny. Cat didn't become a champion racehorse. Instead he became a champion show horse.

⟶ SOLMIR

You certainly couldn't have said he was popular. No one at Johnson and Wales University wanted to ride the big warmblood. Nobody, that is, except Christine.

Solmir was massive. At 17.3 hands, he wasn't just big, but strong as well. And stiff. His long body made him difficult to collect. It wasn't just his build that made him difficult either; it was his temperament as well.

Solmir had been donated to the college because of a mysterious front end lameness. The former Prix St. Georges level horse was now a schoolmaster for students to learn on. That was the plan anyways. The reality was that Christine was the only one who wanted to ride him.

As an upperclassman, Christine was one of the lucky ones who got to try new horses when they came in to see if they were suitable for the program. Despite his size and difficult temperament, the first time Christine rode the huge Swedish Warmblood gelding she knew there was something there. The connection was instantaneous.

For one thing, he was impressive. He had a massive shoulder and a huge neck, yet he wasn't beefy looking. He had an elegant presence.

But it was so much more than that. The more time she spent with him, the more Christine became attached. By the time the school year ended the thought of leaving him behind to return to her home on Long Island broke her heart. She couldn't do it: she was in love.

Fortunately, Johnson and Wales had no summer program, and

therefore allowed students to free lease the horses for the summer. Christine grabbed the opportunity, and took Solmir to her trainer, Luis Denizard's barn for the summer. Luis had just opened his own barn, Delante Stables in Lincoln, Rhode Island, so the timing was perfect.

Christine had never owned her own horse before so she was overjoyed at the opportunity to play the part of horse owner with this horse who consumed her every thought. Shopping was fun. She bought him fly spray, bell boots and of course, lots of treats. Weekends found her working at the barn or taking care of Luis' daughter, to help with the cost of board.

Christine was determined to give Solmir the best possible life. She put him on a joint supplement and did whatever Luis recommended to help him. Turned out daily on 99 acres sprinkled with ponds and accompanied by cows, Solmir was experiencing an entirely new episode in his life.

In the past, Christine had ridden and shown hunters and jumpers. Luis helped her transition to dressage: as Christine says, "totally turning me into a rider." She gives him tremendous credit for their success.

Solmir had been schooled to the upper levels of dressage, so Christine was looking forward to showing him. As she herself was a newcomer, she thought they would be starting at the bottom, perhaps in some training level tests.

So it came as quite a shock when Luis told her that at their first show they would compete at Second level. Well, Christine figured, he was the trainer, so he knew best. It was Second Level that they entered.

The temperature at the show was 98 degrees, so hot that the judges waived jackets. Christine wore hers. It was her first dressage show. She was determined to make a good impression.

She did. She and Solmir won everything. And it was instantly apparent that he loved every minute of it. So Christine found, did she. Her smile as she and Solmir did a knock-em-dead extension across the diagonal could be seen from the arena back to the trailers. Their partnership had developed to yet another level.

The summer was idyllic, but way too short. Soon it was over and Solmir had to return to school. Christine, however, had to leave him behind. She needed to be in New York City to complete her internship at Miller's Saddlery.

She did mention to Beth Beukema, director of Johnson and Wales equestrian program, that if Solmir wasn't working out and they wanted someone to take him off their hands, she would be happy to oblige. In fact, she recalls mentioning that a few times.

When it came time to actually leave Solmir she discovered that it was nothing short of torture. It was their first separation, and it was hard on both of them.

Solmir would go off his feed, and mope. Yet when Christine came for visits, he would go right back to eating. She would run into the barn, calling his name, and the whole barn would hear him scream his greeting to her.

When Christine visited, she would also hear stories about things that Solmir did while she was away. One time a rider was jumping down a line in the indoor arena. At the end of the line, Solmir decided not to turn. Continuing straight ahead, he crashed right into the mirror placed across the short side of the ring. The mirror didn't stand a chance against the huge horse.

Another time, at a dressage show, Solmir decided if he wasn't competing with Christine, well then he wasn't competing at all. Jumping over the chain outlining the ring he took off back to where the trailer was parked.

He was trying hard to tell the world that Christine was his person. Why couldn't they see that?

Christine could see it. She and this horse were meant to be together. Every time she would hear about Solmir's adventures, she would ask Beth. "So when are you going to give me my horse?"

As summer approached once again, relief from the constant separations came in sight. Beth told Christine that she was welcome to lease Solmir for the summer once again.

Christine was thrilled. Immediately, she set out to find a barn near her home, one close enough for her to get to easily yet still affordable. Her job required her to take the train into the city nearly every day, so the barn would need to have night hours.

Christine also began to accumulate the supplies she would need. Fortunately her job at Miller's gave her access to cheap goods. She could go in the warehouse and choose items that were marked down to rock bottom. They might have a disadvantage—Christine was annoyed when she had to get him a blanket in navy and hunter instead of his trademark black and silver colors. But hey, they would survive.

Meanwhile she socked away whatever money she could towards the board.

Summer finally arrived. Christine had made arrangements with a shipper from Maine who would pick Solmir up on his way to New Jersey and drop him off.

She'd even managed to secure a special stall for him. Unlike the other huge barns at Stanhope Farm, this was a separate two stall barn with turnout. Christine didn't want Solmir living in a small stall with limited turnout. He was her soulmate and only the best would do.

Obsession would be a polite way to describe Christine's emotional state. She counted down the days and hours left until Solmir's arrival. The day before he was due, she made all the final preparations. His stall was bedded in a thick mat of fluffy shavings. The stall had been scrubbed, cobwebbed, and the buckets were immaculate. In fact Christine had spent the entire day making everything right for Solmir.

But now he was on his way, and Christine was waiting with her boyfriend Dave at the barn.

The appointed time for his arrival came and went with no sign of Solmir. Christine knew he had been picked up at Johnson and Wales on time. She began to worry.

Finally a call came from the shipper. He had had to pick up another horse and was delayed. "But," he said, "your horse is a saint.

I don't hear a peep out of him. He jumped right on the trailer, and he's calmly eating his hay."

Christine went back to waiting. Impatiently. She'd waited so long! Why was it taking even longer?

Another call came. Now the shipper was stuck in traffic. Again, though he told her her horse was a saint. In fact he said, "he's the best horse I've ever shipped."

Good news, but Christine had long hours of work ahead of her the following day. She had to be in the city in time to open the store and then close it that night. It was now after midnight. She couldn't wait any longer; she had to go home.

The next morning Christine jumped out of bed at 5:30 and she and Dave raced to the barn. When they got there Christine barely waited for the car to stop. She hit the ground running and flew to Solmir's stall, calling him as she ran.

Solmir was bucking and jumping in his stall, screaming to her. "HURRY UP!!!" he seemed to be saying. Running into the stall Christine threw her arms around him and he responded promptly by wrapping his mighty neck around her and holding her close to him. When he let go, he walked in circles around her looking at her as though he couldn't believe she was truly there. Christine burst into tears.

Dave stood with his mouth open, his eyes wide. He could not believe what he had just seen!

It was in May that Solmir arrived at Stanhope Farm. By the end of June he began tripping, tripping badly. Christine already had him on glucosamine and chrondroitin. She didn't know what else to do.

She loved this horse, loved him more than anything in her life. She had to help him; she had to make him better. Yet he wasn't hers, so she couldn't make the decisions. She couldn't stand it.

She called the college. Reaching Beth, she told her what was happening. "I want to call the vets and have him thoroughly examined but he's not my horse. What should I do?"

121

The answer she got brought her to tears.

"I was actually just about to call you, in fact I already sent you a letter. You can consult any vet you want, you can do whatever you would like. Solmir is yours."

Christine took him to New Bolton. Investigation determined that Solmir had a navicular cyst. By following the management and shoeing techniques the vets recommended Solmir returned to soundness. Christine consulted an animal communicator to be sure he wasn't in any pain. He wasn't. But he did deliver some additional information. He considered their relationship to be a marriage. It was no surprise to Christine.

Solmir, now 25, is still the love of Christine's life. But don't tell her husband.

⟿ SYLVESTER

When we go looking for a horse, and locate the one we want, we think "we've found a horse." Sometimes, probably more often than we admit, it's the other way around. A horse discovers that he has "found a little girl."

Sylvester was looking for a new owner. The big grey gelding had been abused, and was leery of people. He was in Laura's barn to be sold.

Laura had acquired Sylvester by chance. She had purchased a horse from a man who had offered her Sylvester as well. Looking into Sylvester's eye, Laura saw beyond the worry: she spotted a genuinely kind soul. Besides, his eyes were beautiful: soulful brown fringed with huge grey lashes. Sylvester came home with her.

Although Ali and Carol, her grandmother, were not in the market for a horse, they had come to Laura's barn with a friend who was. Ali arrived dressed in her riding clothes. When Laura spotted her, she asked Ali if she wanted to ride Sylvester while she waited for her friend. He was a sale horse, she told Ali, and needed to be worked.

Laura knew that Ali, although young, was an excellent rider with a natural feel for a horse.

The combination worked out well: Ali had a great time riding Sylvester. He was fun to ride and eager to please. A huge smile lit her face as she dismounted.

Laura took Sylvester from Ali, who started to walk away to pick something up. To Laura's surprise, Sylvester pulled free of her grasp, went over to Ali, and laid his head on her shoulder. Laura was shocked. Up until now the horse had been very aloof and undemonstrative.

Ali took Sylvester back to the cross ties where she untacked him and put all his gear away. Sylvester never took his eyes off of her. Carol couldn't get over it. She took photos of the big grey horse watching her slight granddaughter's every move.

Carol had been the one who had given Ali her start with horses. When Ali was six, Carol led her around bareback on her own horse, Callie. Soon it progressed to lunge lessons and in no time Ali was fearlessly jumping her grandmother's mare.

Laura couldn't help but be impressed with Ali and Sylvester. She had never seen the horse act this way. Ali, she said, was welcome to ride Sylvester any time she wanted.

Although Ali had been leasing another horse, the horse had gotten injured and she had since been excused from the lease. She had been disappointed, but now her disappointment gave way to excitement. She *would* have a horse to ride, and a very nice one at that!

As Sylvester stood on the ties, Ali handed him a carrot. Sylvester dropped his head, pricked his ears forward and gently took the carrot out of Ali's hands.

Laura did a double take. "Ali, he's never taken treats from anyone!" Sylvester was obviously smitten by the little girl.

Ali took advantage of Laura's offer and rode Sylvester whenever she got the chance for the next two months. Sylvester soon morphed into "Silly" as the horse bloomed in Ali's presence. He relaxed, lost his worried look, and became very affectionate. He followed Ali around like a lovestruck puppy: if Ali walked, Silly walked. If Ali ran, Silly ran. He would lay down next to her and roll over. He was so playful and silly, that the name change just stuck.

It wasn't long before Ali and Silly got the chance to show in a nearby schooling show. They did very well, so well that they beat a professional in a flat class.

Still, Sylvester was for sale. Ali knew that.

Ali and her family weren't the only ones impressed with Sylvester's performance at the show. Someone recognized him from the internet ad that Laura was running. The woman liked what she saw and his success at the show didn't hurt. She was interested in buying him. Very interested in fact. She wanted an appointment to come try him.

Laura knew she had to talk to Ali's mom, Jody as soon as they got home. She couldn't help but see the attachment between Ali and Sylvester and she didn't want to see it end. She wasn't sure if Jody could buy Sylvester, but she had to give her a chance.

Jody appreciated Laura's gesture, but knew she had to talk it over with her husband, Randy. What were they going to do? Randy, like everyone around them, had seen the bond between Ali and Silly. The horse was in love with his daughter. He followed her everywhere. If he was in crossties, his eyes would follow her, and he would step forward in the ties to be sure she never left his sight.

Could they do it? It certainly wasn't in the budget. They knew the responsibilities and financial obligations involved in buying a horse. They discussed every aspect. Finally, Jody went to Laura to find out if she would drop the price. Maybe they could afford him then.

Sadly, the answer was no. "The price is firm," said Laura. "I know he's sound and well worth it."

Now what were they going to do? If they didn't buy Silly, they would break *both* Silly's and Ali's hearts.

Laura did provide a measure of encouragement. She *was* willing to be paid in installments.

Jody and Randy discussed the possibility of a major sacrifice on their part. Perhaps they could take out a home equity loan to buy Silly.

"You can see the love," Randy said. "We can't let him go!"

Jody talked to her parents, explaining what they were thinking of doing. For Carol, the choice was clear. She had dreamed of owning a horse when she was nine. The horse hadn't come. There was no way that was going to happen to her granddaughter. She and Jody's dad were in a position to help, so they did.

The deal was made and Silly was purchased for Ali. Jody bathed Silly until he was spotless and his tail hung down in silky strands. She tied a big blue ribbon around his neck and affixed a card to it.

When Ali arrived, she was confused. "Is it Silly's birthday?" she asked. "What's going on?"

"Read the card," Jody told her.

Ali picked it up. "Woo-hoo!!" it said on the outside. Ali opened it up. Inside, the message was, "Congratulations Ali, you are now Silly's owner."

Speechless, Ali went to Silly's head and gave him a big hug. She whispered "You're mine, buddy."

Silly understood. Relieved, he sighed, dropped his head and buried it against Ali's chest. There was no doubt about the look on his face. It said "I've found my little girl."

BEATING THE ODDS

⤳ Aly Ad Libs

As a yearling the colt, bred and born at legendary Calumet Farm, sold for $185,000 at the elite Fasig Tipton Sale. On the track, he earned $140.

That didn't discourage Pat Garthwaite and Pavel Blaho. The partners own Tatra Farm in Clinton Corners, New York, where they bred and trained both show and race horses. This horse was a son of Alydar, with both Northern Dancer and Native Dancer in his bloodlines; he was bred like royalty. He had only raced two times before being injured. During the recovery his owner died and his future was held prisoner to a probate court.

He wound up at the Saratoga Horses of Racing Age sale as a three year old. Pat and Pavel's agent, Tom Gallo was at the sale. Pavel had told him if he found a nice stallion prospect to call him.

The estate needed to sell the horse. Returned by one buyer, who had paid $27,000, he was available again. The stallion only had one testicle and was a cribber as well.

Pavel, on Gallo's recommendation, decided to buy the horse sight unseen. He offered $2500 cash. The estate, anxious to have the horse off their hands, agreed.

Pavel immediately left for Saratoga to pick their new horse up. Ad Lib is a big, athletic stallion, close to 17 hands. He's not easy to work around and is a known biter. Pavel calmly grabbed a hay string and used it to lead the stallion on to the van while the grooms at the track watched in fear and astonishment. Ad Lib loaded quietly and was soon headed to his new home.

The partners had purchased the horse as a racehorse. His injury was fully healed and with his bloodlines they wanted to have a go at the track. Tatra Farm has a training track on the grounds, so Ad Lib was galloped to get him fit again. Meanwhile, they also popped him over a few jumps. He was sensational.

However, his return to the track, like his first stay there, was short lived. There was a reason his racetrack earnings had only come to $140. His trainer, Dominick Galluscio, called within a week. "He can't run. He's too slow."

Ad Lib came home. He would be a jumper instead.

Jumping, it turned out, was child's play for the stallion. He loved it. He took to it quickly and it was obvious that he was having fun. He was so good that within two years of showing and at the young age of six, he was forced to move up to the Open Division. Pat didn't feel that the young horse was ready to tackle the division, so she carefully chose smaller classes, and did some speed classes with him as well.

Pat marveled at the way her horse jumped. He loved it so much, "it's just play to him, it's never work."

Tatra moved to Ocala, Florida for the winter show season. At these shows, Olympian Dennis Murphy would meet them and he and Pat and Pavel would school together. Dennis met Ad Lib and liked the horse. In fact, he wished *he'd* had him.

Dennis had qualified for the 1998 National Horse Show, then held at Madison Square Garden in the fall, with his Grand Prix Horse Continental B, owned by Lila Lavigne. When a rider qualified a Grand Prix horse, they were allowed to take along a second horse as well to show in the speed classes. Dennis didn't have a speed horse, so Pat offered him Ad Lib.

He came to Tatra at Clinton Corners to work with Ad Lib shortly before the Garden. He was very grateful that the horse was being loaned to him. He knew it was the best horse Pat had ever had in her life and it had to be difficult for her to watch someone else on him. He says, "when you have a great horse like that, it's a little like loaning your spouse to someone else."

He asked Pat to ride first, so he could see how Ad Lib liked to be ridden. Then he got on. He hit it off beautifully with the horse. Ad Lib suited his style of riding and Pat was happy to see how well the two got along.

At the Garden, the stallion was once again an amazing competitor. Dennis said he was "a delight to ride, with a wonderful mouth, and super, super careful." The two placed third in the speed class there against the top horses and riders in the world, and were the highest placed Americans. The yellow ribbon they won is still proudly displayed in the dining room at Tatra.

When he wasn't jumping, Ad Lib was in the breeding shed. He was extremely difficult to manage, very aggressive. Pat says when "you're on his back, he's easy. But on the ground he's a very tough horse to work with, because he always thinks he's breeding."

However difficult he was in the breeding shed, the result was some talented offspring. His first, a filly named Ali Oh Yeah, went to the racetrack and won her first race. She inherited her dad's love of jumping and later became a very successful hunter, showing in a fat snaffle and almost always ending up circuit champion.

Ad Lib and Pat started doing well in the smaller Grand Prix, winning the Saratoga Cup one week, and placing second in the Grand Prix there the second week. When they returned to Ocala the following winter, their successful streak continued.

Competitive success wasn't the only good thing Pat encountered in Ocala. David Towle, who now owns Rio Vista Products, was sponsoring the Grand Prix at Horse Shows in the Sun (HITS) in 2000. The two met and instantly hit it off.

In May of that year, Rio Vista Products sponsored the Grand Prix in Ellenville, New York, the former site of HITS North. Pat and Ad Lib were riding by the tent where David was set up. It was full of people. Ad Lib is an unusual grey, with big, dark blotches on his sides. Pat called into the tent, "Hey Rio Vista guy, look at what your shampoo is doing to my horse."

They were married within two years.

Ad Lib and Pat were on a roll. They had amassed an enviable competitive record, and, even more importantly, they were both having the time of their lives. Pat thought that they would always be together. For this horse, unlike others at the farm, was never supposed to be sold.

That changed when Olympic Bronze Medalist Norman Dello Joio walked into the barn one day. He was looking for a horse for his amateur rider, Toddie Singer. Norman only looked for the best and has high standards. At first he didn't find anything that he thought would do the job. He even walked out of the barn. Pat, watching, breathed a sigh of relief.

But then he turned around and walked back in. Pat held her breath. "What about that grey horse?" he asked. And it was done. It wasn't Pat's choice, but Ad Lib was sold.

Pat was devastated. She loved him like she had never loved another horse.

When the vet came, the pre-purchase exam only took 15 minutes. Pat secretly hoped the horse would fail. That night, she stayed in his stall all night and cried. When Ad Lib left the next morning, she felt like her heart left on the van with him.

But Tatra Farm was a business, and the business had to survive. The amount paid for Ad Lib was significant: enough to pay off some bills and put a downpayment on a 40 acre farm in Ocala (now 60 acres, called Tatra South). A farm in Ocala had always been Pavel's dream. He is now retired there.

Norman had been acting as an agent for Paul Valliere. He trained for Paul at the shows. Paul is banned because of his participation years ago in insurance fraud: killing horses for insurance money.

Pat feels that Paul is extremely remorseful for what he did and is doing everything possible to try to make up for what he has done in the past. When Ad Lib was sold, Pat told Paul, "if it doesn't work out, I would love to have him back. Please make him come back to me." Paul didn't forget.

Toddie and her mom, Ellie Belknap, were both kind people who took good care of their horses. Pat felt at least that he would have a good home where he would be loved and cared for. But that didn't fill the void in her life.

She kept in touch with them to see how Ad Lib was doing. Toddie was showing him in the Children's/Adult Jumpers and doing well.

Then Pat heard the news that there had been some type of injury to his hind foot. It was thought that he had caught it in the rails of his paddock fence. It was reportedly a career ending injury, and Ad Lib was retired to stud in Virginia. He was in great company. One of his stablemates was Saluut.

In time, though, the breeding farm was sold, and no one connected with Ad Lib was informed. The horses had been neglected and all of the stallions except Ad Lib had been removed. The farm was basically abandoned. Pat's horse, the love of her life, was starving and neglected.

Pat was vacationing in Cape Cod with her sister when her phone rang. They were driving down 495, just past the exit for Paul Valliere's barn. The caller was Paul Valliere.

"You can have the gray horse back if you want, but you have to pick him up tomorrow."

Pat couldn't believe it! Her next call was to David. "We're going to Virginia."

She was frantic. She couldn't wait to get to Virginia. The trip seemed endless. But as they pulled into the farm, her excitement turned to dismay. She couldn't believe what she was witnessing: a dilapidated farm, with fences falling down, brush and weeds overtaking the fields.

Then she saw a grey horse in the distance. He was skin and bones, his head hanging. "That can't be him," she told David.

But it was.

Pat was horrified, beyond tears. How could this have happened? "How could I have let this happen to the best horse I've ever had?

He was my best friend, my buddy, my fellow competitor. We were a team."

She walked up to Ad Lib. He picked up his head, shook it up and down a few times and stared at her in recognition. Then he dropped it again, in resignation. Pat hoped she had made it in time: the horse barely seemed to care whether he lived or died.

Untouched by a farrier in months, Ad Lib's feet were starting to curl up. He was so close to death that Pat didn't think he would make it home. She immediately gave him electrolytes and water and got him on the van.

He made it home alive.

Pat called Paul the next day to thank him. If he hadn't called her, her horse would have died. Paul had had no idea how bad the situation was at the farm: no one knew what had gone on or why. He was as shocked by the horse's condition as Pat was.

Toddie and her mother Ellie were also unaware of what had happened, and devastated to think that their horse had been suffering. They, along with Paul, worked out an undisclosed arrangement whereby Pat was once again Ad Lib's owner, but they retained breeding rights.

Pat went right to work resurrecting Ad Lib. A farrier came to correct his feet, and she started walking him daily, beginning with just 10 minutes. It took eight months, and lots of love and care to restore Ad Lib to a healthy condition.

Once Ad Lib was himself again, he went back to work.

The following winter they went to Florida where Ad Lib and Pat did well in the Level six and seven jumpers. In Saratoga that spring they competed in the Saratoga Cup again. But Pat felt her horse was struggling. Although he tried his heart out, she knew it was too much for him. She dropped him back to Levels 5 and 6.

She says she is forever grateful to him for teaching her how to win, and to Pavel as well for teaching them both how to win together.

Ad Lib is now leased to Tatra Farms' working students and his new job is to teach the kids, to help move them up a level. Showing him in the Marshall and Sterling League, the students have been tremendously successful.

Becky Baumel, a student at Findlay College, competed in the Marshall and Sterling Finals with him and showed him at the 2007 Hampton Classic as well, where they placed in every class, one of which had over 70 entries. As Becky is one of Pat's favorites, watching the combination do well is enormously satisfying to her. Ad Lib, says Pat, "has taught Becky how to win."

Pat is also planning to breed Ad Lib more often. Having more of his babies around can only make her happier.

Pat and Ad Lib were meant to be together. Although fate tore them apart, it also brought them back together. Fate was kind enough to give them a second chance. And this time, Ad Lib will stay at Tatra, where he has always belonged.

⟶ IMA GOOD 1-2

On a hotness scale of 1 to 10, he is a 12. He's small at 15.3, but like many short men he's very opinionated. Although he shares his field with a miniature donkey, he thinks he's the big stallion on the farm.

Patty van Housen grew up riding with her sisters at the Milwaukee Hunt Club. Their mother taught them that owning horses was a job, "just like school or work." Although Patty competed in the hunters as a junior and on into her thirties, she switched to jumpers when she realized how much she enjoyed the challenge of "racing against yourself."

Now located in Mequon, Wisconsin, Patty is a safety manager and competes as an amateur. With her sister Barb, she owns a small barn, Split Rail Stable, where they raise babies and retrain off the track Thoroughbreds. The farm is named after the split rail fence that circled her childhood home.

Visitors are often surprised when they don't see a split rail fence at the farm. But, Patty's Dad used to explain, "when you take a closer look, every rail on the farm is split."

One of the highlights of Patty's competitive life was winning the Adult Jumper Finals at the Washington International Horse Show in 1999 on Albie Darned.

But things had changed. Patty wasn't sure if she wanted to jump anymore. Albie had been retired and Patty hadn't been able to find another horse that she could have fun on. Although she loved jumping, she had had several injuries, including a broken jaw and two compressed vertebrae. She had experienced double vision and was having panic attacks. The thought of jumping frightened her. Her confidence was gone and she didn't want to get hurt any more.

That was, until Rodney (Ima Good 1-2) came along. Patty's trainer, Nancy Whitehead, didn't have room for all her horses. She had purchased Rodney off the track. A son of Flying Pidgeon (who had earned over a millions dollars on the track), Rodney was well bred and obviously athletic.

Nancy had seen one of Rodney's relatives, Flying War Hawk (who became very successful in the Jumpers as Crouching Tiger) while teaching a clinic. She was fascinated by his beautiful jumping style, and the way he kicked out behind in the air to avoid touching a rail. She suggested to one of her customers that they look for another off the track Thoroughbred by Flying Pidgeon. They found Madison Bridges, a 16'3 hand gelding with the same jumping style and freaky hind end.

That proved so successful that Nancy went looking for another one. She contacted Jane White, Flying Pidgeon's syndicate manager. Jane helped Nancy get in touch with an owner who had another offspring, Rodemo (derived from Rolf, Edward and Omar, the trainer, owner and exercise jockey) for sale. Nancy purchased the horse, supposedly a 17 hand four year old, sight unseen.

When a rickety Quarter Horse trailer pulled into Nancy's driveway, Nancy was not amused. No 17 hand horse would fit upright into that rig. Nancy and Patty now joke that the track measures "in men's inches and not women's."

Feeling rather irritated, Nancy put a junior rider on him for one of his first rides. For some reason, Nancy put a plank up for the horse to jump. She never does this, feeling that green horses generally jump them terribly. Yet something made her do it. The young horse jumped it amazingly well, both in front and behind. Nancy asked the young girl to take the horse over the plank again. Again he jumped it phenomenally well.

Nancy decided not to do any more. The horse was so wired that she felt he should be turned out for a six month vacation before continuing. Unfortunately, Nancy was in the middle of changing training operations so she needed to place all her horses quickly.

So Nancy asked Patty if she wanted the horse. She thought he would be a good project for her. Nancy had a good feeling about him. She knew he would be difficult, but she could also see he had talent.

There was an additional reason she wanted Patty to have the horse. She was aware of Patty's loss of nerve and was concerned that Patty was about to quit showing jumpers. This horse, thought Nancy, could just be Patty's ticket back to jumping and showing.

Nancy practically begged Patty to take him. "I need a home for him and he's your kind of horse. If you don't take him, I'll have to ship him to Indiana tomorrow." She told Patty about his brilliant jumping style, and said "if you can figure out how to ride him there will be no stopping you."

When Patty said yes, Nancy wasted no time. The horse was on a trailer on its way from Nancy's Illinois location to Patty's Wisconsin farm before Patty had a chance to change her mind. Patty wasn't even at home—he was delivered while she was still at work.

At first, Nancy's good feeling about the horse didn't seem all that accurate. The small bay with the pony face was handsome and well put together, but he was a maniac. He would root and pull and kick. He did levades that would make a Lippizan green with envy. Sometimes he would pin his ears back and give you a look that plainly declared, "you are going to die!" Patty invited other people who came to her farm to ride him but it only took a ride or two before he had spooked them all and there were no takers.

Jumping him was an experience. He would go down to a one foot fence tugging and pulling and then leap over it in a huge arc, rooting as he landed. His stride was tiny from pulling so much. Patty says "his butt was always trying to pass his front end."

To improve his stride and his flatwork, Patty works with dressage trainer Tori Polonitza, of Bonita Springs, Florida. He was so obstinate and violent with his displeasure that Tori once asked Patty why she kept riding him. She answered, "he makes me feel like a kid again. When you jump him he is a blast! He is like driving a little sports car with a huge jump. He can go from 0 to 60 in one stride."

Rodemo was soon renamed Rodney in recognition of the fact that he rides like a hot rod!

Patty is a talented and experienced amateur, yet she still had her hands full working with Rodney. They experimented with many different bits, from bitless to gags to Mikmars. Finally they settled on a small leverage western gag for jumping and a mullen mouth snaffle for every day. Patty says if Rodney is high, she still never knows "if he will leave out two strides at a cross pole" when she is jumping at home." In fact, on days like that, she still "can not believe that I ride him."

In time they went to a little show in Waukesha, Wisconsin. Patty promised Nancy it was "just to school." When Rodney jumped right around in schooling, Patty decided the two foot jumpers might be fun. That went so well they did the 2'6"/2'9" jumpers as well. They ended up Champion in the Low Jumper division. Rodney did his first in and out and his first triple combination, at the show. In addition, it was the first time he cantered a course. He was fearless and competitive and Patty was thrilled.

They moved on, attending more local shows. If things went well, Patty would go on and do the next higher division. Rodney was very consistent and always brought home some ribbons. His aggressive nature made him a fierce competitor.

Patty was soon absolutely smitten with her horse. He is such a confidence builder. She no longer considers giving up jumping; she's having way too much fun!

Before she knew it, Rodney was ready to move to a 3'6" division. Nancy suggested that they go to Lamplight Equestrian Center in Wayne, Illinois, to do the adult jumpers. Patty agreed, but when she took her lesson that week, she kept getting stuck in a corner to a jump going away from the barn. Unable to find a distance, she would pull up.

After Nancy left, Patty freaked out. How could she take that step after a lesson like that? She called her nephew Paul Yanke who had ridden in the Junior/Amateur Jumpers for years with Laura Kraut before going to work for a living. Paul had had a lot of success with some difficult horses, including Player (who was Amateur Jumper champion at the Garden one year) and Skippin School.

Although Paul hadn't done much jumping recently, he took pity on his aunt and agreed to ride Rodney. Patty was unable to watch as she was at work. Nancy recounted the ride to her later on.

When Paul came to the spot in the corner where Patty always pulled, Paul kicked instead. It was a major breakthrough. Rodney's stride and focus instantly doubled and Nancy was astounded at the unbelievable scope she witnessed in the horse.

Off Patty and Rodney went to Equifest 1, an A3 rated show. The first class was on Friday afternoon near dusk. It was a Washington International Horse Show Adult Jumper class. When she walked the course, Patty thought she had lost her mind. The jumps were huge: maximum heights and spreads. Patty wondered what she was doing there.

As they began schooling, Rodney picked up on her nerves. He responded with aggression: rooting, pulling, and kicking up behind. He would twist his butt to the inside so badly on corners that it was almost a right angle. The class was nearing the end and they were calling Patty to the ring. She hadn't even gotten him to the jump in the schooling area.

Nancy asked her if she wanted to scratch.

Patty answered "just set up the jump and let's go to the ring."

Not only did they make it around, they made it to the jump off—and just missed being in the ribbons.

They made it to the jump-offs that weekend in each of their three classes, and earned one eighth place ribbon.

At the last show that summer they competed in the Grand Prix Ring. Every rider was going faster and faster in the jump-off. Patty was in the last group of four to come back to jump off. The last few fences were a big oxer almost in the middle of the ring aimed at the gate, followed by a huge sweeping run to a vertical-vertical two stride in and out going away from the gate. It was 12 to 15 strides from the oxer to the in and out, which some exhibitors jumped as a one stride.

Nancy, who doesn't usually coach from the sidelines, yelled, "You better do something smart," as Patty left the oxer on her way to the in and out. Patty couldn't think what Nancy might mean, so she did the only thing she could think of. Nothing. It worked.

They jumped in big to the in and out, popped out in two and they had won their first A rated class!

Since then, the two have racked up an astounding record. Last year they finished at the top of the North American League Adult Jumper qualifying season with over 1000 points above their closest competitor. (It was the third time they qualified at the top of the leader board.) They also led the qualifying field for the Washington International Horse Show, where they placed 3rd in the finals, and they took 3rd at Harrisburg as well. They led the Marshall and Sterling League qualifiers in 2005 and were second in 2006. The bigger the show, the bigger Rodney gets and the better he performs. Although Patty feels at times like "a pony on parade," Rodney rides like a big horse, with a huge jump.

Along with the awards for competition, Patty won a prestigious award honoring her for her giving nature. Patty is a rider who gives back to the sport, who volunteers her time and resources to help others. In 2006 she earned the United States Hunter Jumper Association Amateur Sportsmanship Award.

Rodney's competitive nature, consistency and bravery have made other exhibitors sit up and take note. They are (including Patty herself, who now owns one of his siblings, Desert Pete) buying up his relatives. Patty, who is extremely appreciative of Nancy's gift to her of Rodney, paid Nancy back in kind. She purchased one of Rodney's sisters, Darling Devil, and gave her to Nancy to breed to her stallion Roc USA.

Darling Devil has proven just as talented as her illustrious family. Her first foal for Nancy, Roulette 22, is doing extremely well in

140

Hunter Breeding Classes and in the International Hunter Futurity.

Rodney started out as a project for Patty. Instead, he proved to be the horse who gave her back her love for jumping, and enabled her to enjoy the thrill of competition once again. He grew from "being a project to being a friend." And along the way he has become Patty's horse of a lifetime.

⤳ Beating the Odds

Michelle Clopp was 10 years old and just learning to ride. She had just begun jumping cross rails so school horses were all she needed. Her mother had no intention of buying her a horse.

Michelle was good and learned quickly. Soon she got an opportunity to ride a private horse, a Quarter Horse cross named Beau, in her lessons. She did well with him. The horse's owner rarely showed up, and it was good for him to get some work. Beau was strong, not one you would normally give to a young child, but he and Michelle got along well.

As Michelle progressed, her instructor decided that she was ready to move up a division at horse shows. Michelle had outgrown cross-rails, now she was ready for the Maiden division. He suggested Michelle take Beau.

Michelle's mother Sandy wasn't too sure. "But shouldn't we call the owner and ask her?"

"Oh, the owner will be fine. She only shows up on his birthday, when she brings carrots for him, and champagne for the barn."

Sandy still wasn't sure, but she agreed.

On the day of the show, the owner, Marian, did in fact show up. It turned out that a relative of hers was the steward. But there wasn't a problem.

"It works out fine for me," she said. "It's good for Beau to be worked. I probably won't ride him again. He's too strong a horse for me."

Beau and Michelle swept the Maiden division, winning everything.

Michelle was doing well in her partnership with Beau and she was very happy to have the horse to ride. But then her trainer left the barn and was replaced with a new one. The new trainer told Michelle that she could no longer ride the horse since she didn't own him. She also said that Beau's owner didn't want Michelle riding him.

Michelle went back to school horses.

When Marian became aware that Michelle was no longer riding Beau, she called Sandy. "Why did Michelle stop riding Beau?" she asked.

Sandy explained about the new trainer.

"Well," said Marian, "I didn't say Michelle couldn't ride him. But what if I sell Beau to you?"

Sandy didn't know what to say. She was not in the market for a horse because she had no way to support one. She knew Michelle's Dad certainly wouldn't spring for it.

"How about $1500?" Marian asked.

Sandy knew that was inexpensive, especially since Beau was a good, sound horse, and he and Michelle made a fine team.

"Well, I'm not looking for a horse," she said. "But let me think it over. Maybe I can get a job."

She knew that Michelle loved the horse. She wanted to encourage her daughter, to be supportive of her desire to ride. So she found a job. She hated the job, but she was determined to let Michelle pursue her passion. She called Marian to talk again.

This time the price had dropped to $1000.

Sandy agreed. She wrote a check for $1000, and then drove to Marian's house to pay for Beau.

When she got to the house, there was yet another price change. Now the cost of the horse was $500. Sandy quietly tore up her check and wrote another one. She didn't know much about buying horses, but she did know that this was not the way things normally went, and she was thrilled with her good luck.

Things got even better when Sandy learned that Beau came complete with his tack, a Baker sheet, and a blanket!!

When Michelle took her next lesson, she came out leading Beau. The trainer looked shocked. Sandy explained to her, "You can send the bills to me now. We bought him."

Marian died six months after Sandy purchased the horse for Michelle. It turned out that she had lowballed the price since she knew that she was terminally ill. She wanted to be sure that when she died Beau would have a good home.

Beau was not fancy, and he was strong, but he was consistent and a good jumper. He took Michelle's show career from Maiden (a beginner level in hunt seat equitation) to Medal/Maclay classes (the top level of equitation in hunt seat). The ribbons along the way were innumerable. At one show, Michelle and Beau won so many classes that the announcer started his results with "Guess there's no surprise, but the winner is Michelle Clopp." Even today, as a successful professional, no horse Michelle has ever owned has brought her more success.

Beau was also the most drug tested horse on the circuit. The stewards were sure that such a small child could not handle such a powerful horse unless he was drugged.

Sandy and Michelle were lucky, too for Beau was an amazingly easy keeper. He never had a sick day in his life until the very end. So not only was he cheap to buy, he was inexpensive to maintain.

Michelle showed Beau throughout most of her years as a junior. They rarely returned from a show without at least one blue ribbon. One day she and Sandy made a surprising discovery: Beau was actually 26, not 16 as they had been led to believe.

He didn't seem to be having any difficulty with the 3'6" fences that Michelle jumped in the open equitation division. But Michelle's trainer was worried that Beau's stride had gotten shorter, and that he could no longer get the distance in the in and outs ("related" fences that are separated by just one or two strides).

Michelle knew there was no way she would ever sell Beau. She couldn't do that to a horse that had done so much for her. Beau was still sound and happy, and loved to show. He just needed to do something different, a little easier.

So Michelle leased him, and the legacy continued. The woman who leased Beau showed in the adult amateur hunters, a three foot division, where Beau's beautiful jumping style made him very successful. They went on to win many classes together.

Beau lived to be 38. Michelle would still ride him back and forth to the paddock, hopping on bareback with just a halter.

Then one week, he colicked every night. The vet told them that Beau's systems were shutting down. Michelle had no choice but to put him down.

If you want to purchase a Medal/Maclay horse today for your son or daughter, you could very easily spend well over $100,000. A top hunter can go for up to nearly a million.

Beau really did beat the odds. A one in a million horse, purchased for a bargain basement price, he took Michelle from a rank beginner, all the way to the top. For a struggling mother and her horse crazy daughter, Beau made dreams come true.

⟶ Blondy's Dude
Two Dudes in Cowtown

By Lesli Krause Groves
(Reprinted courtesy of the Quarter Horse Journal)

January 1962. As Morgan Freeman eased the borrowed pickup and trailer onto the black ice that covered the pavement in northeastern Oklahoma, he wondered if it was just a dude's dream to take his stallion to the Forth Worth Fat Stock Show. But if Blondy's Dude could be in the top 10 at Cowtown, it would make a great story to tell visitors at his feed store in Skiatook.

Freeman, 48, had only been to Forth Worth once before. Back in 1941, he'd seen Wimpy named grand champion, then followed other horsemen to the Blackstone Hotel for the first meeting of the fledgling AQHA.

A lot had changed in 21 years.

He found the new show grounds, but then realized he'd forgotten to bring "Dude's" health papers. He yanked off Dude's blankets, then staked him out on a grassy median near the carnival and went off in search of a veterinarian. He saw license plates from states he'd never even visited, the grandest trucks and trailers imaginable. His confidence ebbed when he heard a passerby say there were 795 Quarter Horses entered; it would be the largest show in the breed's history.

Dude had left Skiatook wrapped up like a grandbaby going out to play in the snow. Along the way, his hair had turned every direction under two layers of blankets and a hood. As they headed south into warmer weather, sweat started to slowly trickle down his

146

legs. So while staked on the median, Dude's hair dried in the sun, cementing itself out of place. Freeman returned to find a horse who looked starched, but not ironed.

Now what was he going to do? Dude was just recovering from a cold. Did he dare bathe him? A goose egg had come up on the sorrel's neck where the veterinarian at home had given him a shot. Freeman thought he could hide it by strategically combing his mane, but the mane now had a stubborn mind of its own.

He found a water hose and soaked the sorrel horse, then scavenged around for something to squeegee the water off. He found a piece of broken glass lying on the ground and started using that. An exhibitor stalled nearby walked over and silently handed him a scraper.

His confidence still hadn't returned by the time the 30 aged stallions were called into the arena. Several in the class had established reputations, and their owners and handlers had even greater acclaim. Dude's thin little halter made out of bridle rein leather looked meager now, and the twin imitation silver buckles looked cheap.

Judge Ernest Browning's first move was to jerk his thumb toward Dude, gesturing him out of the line-up. Freeman was shocked. He thought they'd been the first one culled. He wanted to say, "Wait! This is the reigning champion of the Tulsa State Fair!"

"Trot him!" the judge said curtly.

Ah! So they weren't out of the running yet! They took off in a straight line, Dude jerking and bouncing more than trotting. But when the ranks thinned to the top 10 he was still a contender. Browning lined up the finalists with Dude at the end. Tenth was great, thought Freeman. That's the most he'd ever expected. Then they started announcing the winners: 10th, 9th, 8th. Slowly it dawned on Freeman that they were going in ascending order, and Dude's name hadn't been called yet. Then there it was: "First place goes to Blondy's Dude."

While Freeman was still deciding whether he was dreaming or awake, the other class winners came in for the championship drive. Among them were Leo San Siemon, which Freeman knew had been grand champion almost every time he'd been shown.

When the judge told Freeman to trot his horse, he added, "in a circle this time." Freeman was already off in another bouncy sprint before the command registered, but as soon as he turned Dude into the circle, the stallion slowed down, leveled out and traveled like a champion.

"Make him reserve," the judge said, pointing to Leo San Siemon. "Make him grand." he concluded, pointing to Blondy's Dude.

⟶ Tweetie Man

In a world populated by Arabs, Tweetie Man stands out. A big, lanky Thoroughbred, he looks like he showed up at the wrong venue, victim of a mistaken turn on a road trip.

Yet there is no mistake. Tweetie Man has proven he belongs here. With consistent top ten finishes in endurance rides, he's a contender.

When most people decide they would like to do endurance rides they start by buying an endurance horse. Then they learn the sport of endurance riding.

Dave Owens started with a horse: a horse that nobody wanted, one who had no idea what his job was in life, and discovered endurance riding.

Dave was a newcomer to the horse world when he and his wife Darrah purchased Tweetie Man. Recommended to them by a trainer they knew, the four year old Thoroughbred had only been broken for racing when he found his way to their home.

Darrah was experienced with hunters and jumpers, so the idea initially was for Tweetie to become her horse. He proved quite difficult, often spooking and bucking. So Dave and Darrah searched for a trainer who would get along well with Tweetie. They found one, and Tweetie had some success at a horse show, coming home champion.

But at the next show, he tripped in the sand and fell down. Later, when a groom was leading him, he fell down again.

His show career came to a sudden halt.

Despite a lot of testing, it wasn't clear if Tweetie had Lyme or EPM, or both. Nothing was ever firmly diagnosed, but Tweetie obviously had physical problems, so he was treated for both diseases. His physical symptoms were inconsistent: there were days when he seemed to be getting better, days when he seemed much worse. His behavior changed, too—he became very aggressive, attacking people if they came out to his field. Even when he physically seemed well enough to work again he proved he was in no mood mentally by dumping one trainer and then running her over.

Unsure of what to do next, Dave and Darrah decided to give the big horse some time off. He was turned out for a long time, nearly a year and a half. About the end of this period, Dave's own horse became lame. As Dave wanted a horse to ride and Tweetie wasn't doing anything, he decided to give him a try. Tweetie appeared to be sound now, after his rest and the treatments.

Dave had attended a John Lyons clinic and found the work fascinating. During the clinic, he learned how to work horses properly in a round pen.

Since Tweetie had shown significant behavioral problems, Dave felt the round pen work might help him improve. Besides, he wanted to gain some experience with the new skills he had learned, and Tweetie would be a good guinea pig. No one could do anything with the horse until his behavior improved, so it was a necessary first step.

Tweetie proved a surprisingly apt pupil, very willing and taking eagerly to the work. He was working so well that Dave thought he might try riding him. But he was nervous. Tweetie had bucked off a lot of people, many of them far more experienced than Dave was. Dave wasn't sure he would be able to ride this wild horse. Fearing he was over his head he decided he should let someone else work with Tweetie.

He gave the horse to a trainer who was looking for an event horse. Tweetie was very athletic, with a huge stride, and had proved himself a capable jumper. Maybe eventing would prove to be his niche.

It turned out to be a bad move, one that, in retrospect, Dave kicks himself for. Tweetie lost ground. When the trainer came to try him, Tweetie wasted no time dumping him.

Dave said, "Are you sure you want to take him?"

"Sure," the trainer answered.

Dave checked his email one day and there was a message from the trainer. He'd gotten a new bit to try on Tweetie. Dave wasn't sure he liked the idea.

Then Dave got a call while he was vacationing with his family in Martha's Vineyard. "I can't ride this horse" the man said. The trainer hadn't listened to Dave's advice or paid any heed to the work that Dave and Tweetie had done together. So the horse had reverted to his former self, a bucking bronc, and had launched the trainer several more times.

Tweetie came home. Dave promised him, "OK Tweetie, you're my horse now; I'm not sending you away again."

Tweetie relaxed in his field for a month, and then they returned to the round pen work. Dave saddled up his horse and free lunged him in the pen. Tweetie went ballistic, bucking for fifteen minutes with all the ferocity of a rodeo star.

"I'll *never* get on that horse!" thought Dave.

The next day, they did the same thing. Again, Tweetie was a wild bronc.

"A week," thought Dave. "I'll give him a week."

The next day, Tweetie trotted around, trotted to the fence, then back to Dave. He stopped, and put his head down.

"You're going to let me get on you, aren't you?" Dave asked his horse.

And he did.

He was good, too. Dave worked him at the walk using the John Lyons style reining techniques he had learned. He taught Tweetie to move his hips to each side, to move his shoulders to each side, and to give to the bit and relax his neck. For a week, Dave rode Tweetie only in the round pen. But he knew they couldn't stay there forever.

On the day Dave decided to leave the ring and attempt a trail ride, he was scared. He had no idea what the horse would do. But out they went, and Tweetie tore through the woods, scrambling up hills and racing through the flat stretches. It was terrifying—yet, exhilarating, too.

In August of that year, Dave saw an article on competitive trail riding and endurance riding. It sounded quite interesting. It might be something he and Tweetie could do together. He didn't think Tweetie would be a star, what with his unlikely conformation and breeding. Tweetie was a large Thoroughbred, topping out at about 17 hands. And his feet were not the best, with a tendency to crack and break up. But why not try it? Maybe they could finish in the middle of the pack somewhere.

For three months, Dave and Tweetie worked four to five times a week, for one and a half to two and a half hours a day. Sometimes they went out on trail; other days they stayed in the ring and trotted laps, or practiced the reining techniques.

Then they entered their first competition, a competitive trail ride. They came in eleventh, winning the Rookie award.

Dave was surprised and extremely pleased.

One of the things that attracted Dave to endurance rides was the atmosphere. It was nothing like the stressful horse shows that he attended with his wife. Here riders showed up, camped with their horses, and got to enjoy nature. This was something he could get into!

They tried another ride. This time they took second! What a bonus. Dave never even planned to be in the running, and here they were, second! Dave was surprised again, and very proud of his horse. He says, "There is no reason for Tweetie to be successful—but he is!"

Dave decided to learn all he could about the sport, to educate himself so that he could give Tweetie every chance to succeed. At first it was haphazard, but then Dave learned about the Eastern Competitive Trail Ride Association and promptly joined. The newsletter proved invaluable, giving Dave advice on how to train, what to feed and how to monitor fitness.

Dave learned fine tuning at the rides themselves, from speaking with other competitors. Their willingness to share their techniques delighted him. One of the important tools they used was a heart monitor. More than half of the competitors were using them.

Dave tried one, but learned that he was more comfortable trusting his own judgment, relying on feel to determine how much he could push his horse.

At the next ride, Dave and Tweetie came fifth.

They were ready now, Dave felt, for a fifty mile ride. So they tried one, and finished 15th, a very respectable placing for the novices.

There was one last ride for that season. They finished in the top 10.

It was exhilarating. Tweetie Man was a horse nobody wanted; no one even knew if he would ever be sound again. No one thought he had potential for anything, with his health problems and bad attitude. And yet here he was proving to be not only competitive, but a star.

Dave became a student of endurance rides, getting a better feel for conditioning, for strategy. "The whole thing is like a question mark, a mystery that you're always trying to solve." he says.

He soon learned that he was overconditioning, and cut back to three days a week. They spent a lot of time trotting, although Tweetie would mix things up and throw in some cantering too. Since Tweetie was very comfortable that way Dave let him use his own judgment.

To compete in endurance events, riders need to be able to gauge their speed, and the amount of distance they've covered. Dave used a GPS system during training to get a feel for these figures. On a competitive trail ride, distances are marked, so it helps riders learn to feel where they are in the course.

Endurance rides are divided into three legs (marked by vet stops), and riders know how long each leg is. They are not, however, split up evenly. At the holds, horse and rider get rehydrated, with water and electrolytes, and energized with energy foods. Some riders carry food and water for themselves, as well as electrolytes for their horses.

After each ride, Tweetie got a lot of time off. Dave followed the rule of thumb for endurance competitors: a day off for every ten miles of competition.

Dave and Tweetie soon cut down their conditioning even more. In fact, Dave says, "some horses, once they're in shape, they're in shape. They need no more conditioning."

Tweetie "gets cranked at competitions. He's very competitive and is eager to pass everyone. Yet he realizes his limits and knows when he needs to slow down." And Dave has developed a better feel himself now. He knows when he can push Tweetie for just a little more, and when he needs to let him recuperate a bit.

One of the challenges of endurance rides is that each one has its own set of hazards, so there is always something different to figure out. The first ride for Dave and Tweetie in their second year of competition was in Georgia, a 50 mile endurance race. The terrain was flat and sandy, easy on the horses' feet. But there were holes in it, so you had to ride carefully. One team encountered a hole and fell right in front of Dave and Tweetie.

They finished 25th on the ride. Equipment problems plagued them, as Dave tried to figure out the right combination of saddle and saddle pads. Fit is absolutely crucial when riding long distance. The wrong equipment causes rubs, sores, and sore backs.

The next ride was a competitive trail ride where Tweetie and Dave placed 19th. Then it was on to East Cranbury, New Jersey, and another ride featuring flat, hard packed sand as the footing. Challenges here included moguls (not only a hazard for skiers!) and deep puddles, where what was lurking at the bottom was a mystery—until you were in it. They finished this ride in sixth place.

Then it was on to the Sand Hills Stampede in South Carolina. The challenges here included deep, tiring sand, and long, tiring hills. Dave and Tweetie got lost, another hazard of an endurance ride, and had to start over, an hour late. Still, they finished in 11th place, and closed on several horses at the end of the ride. Dave figured out that, had they not gotten lost, they would have been fourth!

He gives all the credit to his horse, insisting "It's all Tweetie!" Dave has worked on becoming a better rider, hoping to help Tweetie any way that he can. His balance in the saddle has improved, which has a significant impact on his horse's ability to carry him for long distances. "Everything," Dave says, "seems to be coming together!"

A totally different course presented itself for the Vermont Bare Bones 50. This race was all about roughing it. A lot of it took place on hard roads, and it was very up and down, with several long inclines. They placed eighth.

Then it was off to Pennsylvania for the Mishaux. There were some very big rocks to contend with in this challenging course. Besides the boulders, many of the trails were pockmarked with smaller rocks creating slow, tricky going. In between there were long stretches of power line trails. Time could be made up here in the nice, grassy footing. But not too much—because there were also a lot of steep hills in the power lines.

For the first 25 miles, Tweetie and Dave dueled with the lead horse. Then they dropped back a little, engaging in a three way battle for second place. Dave was so satisfied with how Tweetie was going that he decided to back off and let Tweetie slow down a little. When a shoe started to come off, Dave got off and walked. Despite the shoe, despite the fact that Dave deliberately decided to back off, they finished sixth. Dave was astonished. He looked at Tweetie. "Who are you?" he asked.

He says "This horse is giving so much above and beyond what he's ever been asked for." All Dave ever wanted, he says "was to go camping with my horse."

Tweetie and Dave finished their second season in ninth place for the Northeast Region, an astonishing finish for a big Thoroughbred and his rookie owner. Dave looks back over the past few years in amazement and says, "I'm still not sure it was Tweetie and I who did this."

⟶ Bethesda After Dark (Shadow)

At 40, Scott Monroe knew nothing about horses. His wife was a pleasure rider; Scott was more interested in horsepower than horses. But a neighbor, Charlie Kellogg kept asking Scott, "Why don't you come for a drive with me? I think you'll like driving and love horses."

Scott took Charlie up on his offer. He found the carriages interesting: he could compare their structure with cars. And he discovered he *did* like driving. So he learned how to drive. Next he learned how to ride. Now he can't get enough of either.

Always athletic and competitive, Scott soon found he wanted someone to judge his driving, to see how he stacked up against others. He started competing in pleasure driving events, but quickly found that they weren't challenging enough for him.

When he learned about combined driving he decided that it might suit his personality a bit better. Purchasing a 16.1 hand Advanced Level horse (a *hot* Advanced Level horse) he competed at Training and Preliminary. When he had to put her down (she was in her twenties) he leased a pair of Arabs to drive. But he knew it was only temporary. He wanted a horse of his own again, a horse that could take him to the top.

At a party, when a friend of Scott's asked him, "What is your dream horse?" Scott described an athletic, hot, gutsy horse. The friend said "That horse is for sale up in Massachusetts."

That horse turned out to be Shadow (Bethesda After Dark), a three year old Morgan who had come from out west. Scott liked that: Morgans from that area were bigger boned than the ones raised in the Northeast. He bought Shadow on the spot. The solid black, 15.2 hand gelding from the Wyoming Flyhawk lines, was "built for the job."

Although people warned Scott that this was not the right horse, that the line was very hot, Scott knew exactly what he wanted. This *was* the right horse: "tough, one with grit."

Employing Margaret Beeman, a local trainer who works with natural horsemanship, to help him with Shadow, Scott began preparing Shadow for his competitive career.

Margaret asked her new client what his goals were with his horse. Scott's reply? "My dream has always been to be on a United States Equestrian Team. And why be on a team if you're not going to win?"

For the first two years they worked on ground work, spending countless hours in a round pen. Thanks to Margaret's work, Shadow's toughness was channeled into confidence: he got braver and bolder. Margaret also became Scott's navigator: timing, and making sure all four wheels of the carriage stayed put on the ground.

Scott was amazed and inspired by what developed through that groundwork. Starting as a rank amateur with a green horse, Scott sound found himself able to stop, turn, back up and transition Shadow through different gaits while Shadow was at liberty in the pen. It was "a real thrill" for him as well as good training for both of them.

Together Scott, Shadow and Margaret, began to rise through the levels. At Training they did five events and won them all. At Preliminary they won five out of six, coming in second in the other. Scott feels that working together from the beginning with his horse is what forged the strong bond that is so evident between them.

Combined driving consists of three phases: dressage, marathon and cones. Combined driving horses have to be "great dancers" on Friday, have incredible wind and strength for the marathon on Saturday, and be able to be a sound and attentive sprinter on Sunday in the cones phase.

Scott says that everything you do at Training Level you do at Advanced; you just have to do it better. For example when Scott was learning Training Level, he was working on getting a good quality two beat trot. At Advanced, that two beat trot has to be developed to include collections and extensions.

Dressage is, as in ridden dressage, about suppleness and collection. A horse doing combined driving must have the muscle to carry himself on his hindquarters during the dressage test, pulling 400-600 pounds of carriage and yet still look light and elegant.

The marathon is 20 kilometers long with up to eight hazards. The time cannot be exceeded, nor can you come in too fast. Drivers receive penalty points for errors or time faults, so the goal is to have the lowest score. It is, Scott says, "grueling. It's about raw strength." Yet in the seven or eight years they've been competing, they have only lost the marathon phase four times. Shadow loves the marathon. "Let me at it!!! I'm *bad*, let me go!" He is, says Scott, "just a brute when he gets out there."

The cones phase is a test of speed and precision. The cones have balls on top, and the distance between the cones gets tighter and tighter as you go up the levels. Each ball that is knocked off incurs three penalty points. In order to win this phase, drivers not only have to navigate the tricky cones, they also have to do it faster than any of the other competitors!

To compete in this demanding sport, horses must be properly conditioned all around: muscles, heart and bone. Scott is lucky: his home in Sharon, Connecticut is surrounded by 1000 acres of trails to work in. But it's not only physically fit; the horses need to be mentally and emotionally fit as well. Scott had to be sure that Shadow, a very intelligent horse, was mentally challenged as well as physically.

Scott says Shadow "loves it, he's a tiger, a horse and a half!"

Shadow is not just an amazing athlete, but he also has his own game plan for competitions. He knows how much energy it takes to compete, so, in order to conserve his energy, he naps in between phases at the shows.

Scott loves the energy at a horse show. There's a lot of camaraderie: good positive energy, good friends, good times and the trading of secrets. Of course, that's after the show day. The next day, during the show, they are all "fierce competitors" again.

They were so successful that in 1999 the United States approached Scott to compete in the Worlds Singles Championship in the Advanced division. Scott had been preparing for that invitation since Day 1. But he knew they weren't ready. Not yet. The move to Advanced is a huge one.

Still, he was honored. He hadn't asked to move up to Advanced. They had asked *him*.

What Scott and Shadow were doing was laying the ground work. Scott had been working on that before anyone knew who he was. He had a goal, and an agenda. Scott owns a tree business in Connecticut, Monroe Tree Service, and he looked at driving the same way. In business you need to have a business plan. To make it to the top in driving, you had to have a plan, too.

Scott knew it was a long process, but he had it all laid out. Each component: riding, driving, conditioning was all part of the program and all laid out each week. Shadow had been purchased when he was three, but they hadn't competed until he was five. They learned everything together. Initially Scott didn't even know what the movements he and Shadow were doing were supposed to feel like. He learned.

He also knew when it was time to move up, something he advises other drivers who he works with to follow. "When you are consistently in the top three of your class, then you can consider moving up." And when you do, know that you are going to drop way back in the placings.

In 2000, when they did make the move to Advanced, they dropped back from winning everything to the middle of the pack. Well, they started in the middle of the pack. Since then they've figured it out. In 2005 and 2006 they were United States National Champions and were chosen Horse of the Year by the United States

Equestrian Federation for the single combined driving horse of the country; in 2004 they were selected for the USEF World Singles Driving Team. When Scott got the news he was "ecstatic!" I was like a little kid—all the hard work, frustration and money that goes into it, it's all paying off." They were the highest placing Americans at the event.

In 2006, they were selected again. Shadow, as a member of the High Peformance Group, even has his own passport!

Combined driving is a very expensive sport requiring two vehicles, two sets of harness and a big enough trailer to haul it all. Each show costs thousands of dollars. Scott is an amateur, competing against professionals. Yet the record that Shadow and he have accumulated speaks volumes about their relationship.

Shadow is more of a "people" horse than a "horse" horse. "He's a loner; he doesn't need other horses." He's very confident in himself and doesn't want to be bothered with other horses. His intense personality mirrors Scott's. His wife Diane says about them, "Scott is Shadow and he's Scott."

Scott says, "I don't think it could be any closer, our relationship. I know everything about him." Last fall, in Italy, (at the World Championships) Scott and Shadow went overseas a week early. The night before they were to leave to go to Rome, they all went out to dinner. Scott went back afterwards to do night check. The barn manager told him Shadow was fine; he was just resting.

One look at his horse told Scott that that was far from the truth. Shadow in fact had shipping fever. Scott stayed with him all night running fluids. Luckily, he was fine and they were able to compete. But they are so connected that it only takes one look in Shadow's eyes for Scott to read him and know what is going on. Are his eyes soft? Or does he look worried?

Horses, Scott says, are "honest every day. They give us as much as they can, and they appreciate us trying to understand them." They "don't judge us. It's a relationship not comparable to anything else; it's like "your best human friend times two."

Although Scott Monroe came to horses later in life than a lot of us, he has more than made up for lost time with his amazing relationship with Shadow. He says, "I'm still excited! I can't believe this is me and this is what we've done. I've got such an incredible horse!"

➷ WHIZARDS BABY DOLL

Audiences around the country are amazed by their virtuoso performances of skill and harmony. Not only do they win top reining events, they do it in a way never done before. Whizards Baby Doll and Stacy Westfall perform without benefit of saddle or bridle.

Stacy had trained Boot Scootin Dolly, (Whizards Baby Doll's mom), and had purchased her first son. With Dolly, Stacy won her first reining money. She got along well with the mare, a horse that hasn't responded as well to other trainers. Dolly, says Stacy, would hold a grudge. "Don't push me," she would tell you. If you did, Dolly's cooperation would end.

Whizards Baby Doll (Roxy) was Dolly's second baby. Stacy and her husband couldn't afford to buy Roxy. Well aware of her talent, they recommended one of their clients, Greg Gessner, buy her. He did.

Stacy first laid eyes on Roxy when she was two days old; she didn't start working with her until she was two years old. Now six, Roxy stays in training with Stacy, but goes home to Greg for a few months for winter vacation.

In 2003, Stacy performed her first bridleless freestyle on Can Can Lena. They were the first ones to compete this way in the National Reining Horse Association Futurity. Others had tried it, using neckropes or sticks, but Stacy was the first to do a true bridleless performance. It was a sensation. Spectators and competitors couldn't stop talking about it.

Then the question came up, "How are you ever going to top that?"

Stacy knew how she could top it. She would ride without a saddle.

Anyone the least bit familiar with reining knows just how challenging the concept of doing a reining pattern bareback is. Lose your balance and you're gone: you can't grip with your legs because you will be miscuing your horse.

Stacy had to physically condition herself in order to be able to reach her goal. She spent that winter riding bareback, doing anything she could to improve her balance, including jumping bareback. She rode until her body hurt everywhere. The feeling in her body was as though she had been doing squats for half an hour. Stacy knew that she had to teach herself to be perfectly balanced and still in order to be able to pull it off.

Of Roxy, she says "she's brainwashed because she doesn't know that she could get rid of me!"

To get to the point of communication that she and Roxy have achieved takes a terrific amount of trust. The trust is gained through hours spent together, trail riding, practicing natural horsemanship techniques, and doing many different activities together. And, Stacy emphasizes, it must be achieved fairly. If you put in the wrong pressure, you confuse the horse, and can cause them to hold grudges.

To begin the process, Stacy worked on getting Roxy as light and responsive as possible. First she would ride with very loose reins, then progress to tying the reins to the saddle horn, again very loosely. She would move her upper body the way she would use it when she had no reins at all. Then she would use the bridle only to make corrections, until she could ride for weeks without using a bridle.

It took Roxy two years to get to the point where she could go bridleless, and another year to where they could perform without a saddle. A level of communication that deep takes a long time to develop.

A lot of the cues Stacy uses are in her legs, so she would make corrections with them. To speed up she uses more leg, to slow down, she softens them and to stop she totally releases them, as though she were taking her foot off the gas pedal.

Stacy knew from the very start that she wanted to spend her whole life with horses. At six, she got her first pony, Midnight Mist. The fact that she had just fallen off a neighbor's pony the day before and broken her arm in no way soured her enthusiasm. Misty, who was purchased for a penny (including saddle and bridle), became her constant companion. The two did everything they could together, showing in every class they could possibly enter, and exploring endless trails. Misty was 16 when she came to Stacy, and lived until the nice old age of 32.

At 14, Stacy started her first "project" horse, a $150 colt. She totally immersed herself in natural horsemanship, watching, reading and learning everything she could.

Stacy was unfamiliar with reining until she went to college. She and her mom (a fellow horse lover) went to the University of Findlay in Ohio to check it out. As Stacy's family was originally from Maine, they arranged to visit an alumnus there who hailed from their neck of the woods. The woman was in Columbus, and the Quarter Horse Congress just happened to be in progress.

Stacy was amazed at the size of the event, it was HUGE! As she walked around she heard the roars of the crowd in the stands and decided to see what was going on. Climbing the stairs into the bleachers, she peeked into the ring. What she saw stopped her in her tracks: a reiner was spinning his horse. It was love at first sight. She knew this was something she had to do.

Stacy had competed in contests such as barrel racing and pole bending, and enjoyed the speed. Reining had speed, but it also had control. It was a wonderful blend: exciting and yet exacting.

The Congress was not only the place where Stacy met her future discipline; it also had another wonder in store for her. It was where she met her future husband, Jesse Westfall, who is a NRHA judge. He happened to be working for a trainer there.

Stacy's first go at reining without tack was at Tulsa, Oklahoma. She was competing against the top reining trainers in the world. Schooling before the class, they all looked at her as if she was crazy. What was she doing at this top notch competition, with no tack? Then she won.

She wasn't crazy anymore. Jesse overheard a wizened old cowboy walking by with one of the other exhibitors. Talking to his companion, the cowboy said, "That girl just whipped your butt and she didn't even have a bridle or a saddle!"

Freestyle reining allows for any kind of artistic impression. Riders design it using their horses' strongest maneuvers. A program is constructed to build slowly: it shouldn't be rushed through. The elements must concur with the music: for example horse and rider burst into spins where the movement in the music bursts, pace picks up when the music picks up. Stacy adds her stops at the end because they are the hardest things to do tackless and what the audience most wants to see.

She loves the freestyles, loves the electricity and the anticipation of the crowd.

The first freestyle she did with Roxy was done to "A Moment Like This." The vision of Stacy attired in her wedding gown on the solid black horse was breathtaking.

She chose "Live Like You Were Dying" to use for the tackless freestyle because it fit so perfectly. She was doing something that had never been done before, taking a big chance.

Stacy sees herself as a bridge between high level horsemanship and natural horsemanship, two entities that unfortunately sometimes seem to be in opposing camps. People in the high level performance classes can at times seem to view their horses as nothing more than a mechanical medium to achieve their end. Natural horsemen may go to the other extreme, acting as though any exertion on the horse's part is akin to abuse.

Stacy believes in a balance. A horse in the upper levels of competition is a conditioned athlete, and yes, he's going to have days when his muscles are sore from exertion. But these horses are cared for extremely well, and most love their jobs. By using natural horsemanship techniques to train them, lighter, more responsive horses are produced with less stress.

Stacy and Roxy are living proof that the two camps can mesh and produce the best of both worlds.

It's obvious from their relationship that Roxy is no "mechanical medium" to Stacy. Her funny, mischievious nature endears her to Stacy. While Stacy's first bridleless horse was serious (Stacy said if she had a voice it would be one of a British nanny) Roxy is known as Foxy Roxy. She is quite impressed with herself. She behaves, but she's always thinking.

Some people watching Stacy and Roxy perform have gathered the erroneous impression that Roxy is a robotic animal who has memorized a pattern which can only be performed within the confines of an arena. Nothing could be further from the truth. Stacy can ride Roxy tackless anywhere and everywhere: the routine works because of the level of understanding that they have.

Another misconception Stacy battles is that people think Roxy behaves because she has been literally worn into submission. She combats this idea by allowing Roxy to run free before some performances. Roxy is let into the arena first, and runs, bucks, twists and kicks at liberty. Then Stacy enters. Roxy walks up to her, and kneels down so Stacy can mount. They then perform their program. At the end, Stacy stands on her horse. Then she gets off and lets Roxy run free once more.

There's no mistaking it. This horse is not tired! She is full of life and energy, and full of the desire to please her rider. She "has all this expression" and yet is willing to be a partner.

At the Quarter Horse Congress last year Stacy showed her in a class that she entered specifically for schooling. Roxy was fresh and Stacy rode her on a ridiculously loose rein. Yet she performed beautifully. In fact they placed in the class even though they were just schooling.

When they came out, Stacy dismounted. After that perfectly controlled performance, Roxy, full of energy, piaffed, tail up in the air. She understands what she is supposed to do, and where and when to do it.

Stacy and Roxy are showing the world that there are no boundaries as to what can be achieved between horses and humans. Their level of communication and trust have raised the bar for horsemen everywhere.

WHOOPS!

⤳ A Judge's Life

Canadian winters are cold. Brutal in fact. Below zero temperatures, freezing winds, mountains of snow.

It was no wonder that judge Randy Roy was looking forward to an escape. He would be judging a horse show at Tropical Park Racetrack in Miami, Florida. He couldn't wait. He would be going to a lush green landscape free of snow, warmed by the hot, hot sun.

Arriving at the show, he checked in with management, gathered up his clipboard and judge's cards and walked over to the ring where he would be judging. The warm Florida sun was such a relief. He just wanted to soak it all up, grab every ounce of it and store it.

The ring was all prepared for him with a judge's booth for him to sit in. But that wouldn't do. Shade from the sun was the last thing he was looking for. So he grabbed a chair and headed to the other side of the ring. There he placed it squarely in the sun and sank into the blissful warmth of the spot. He noticed the pond behind him but thought nothing of it.

Randy was so thankful to be here. What a welcome change from his bitterly cold home. "How much better can it get?" he thought.

The first class began. It was a Low Hunter class, one of those classes that draws a million entries and goes on endlessly. Randy was totally relaxed, soaking up every ray of sunshine and utterly enjoying the heat. Margie Goldstein was on course, and Randy was enjoying her round.

Then a voice came over his walkie talkie: the voice of the announcer. The announcer was located in a tower, affording him a view of the show grounds that no one else had.

"Randy," said the announcer, "Something has gone wrong. Don't make any quick moves."

Randy wondered what possibly could have gone wrong. The first class was in progress: it wasn't even pinned so what could possibly be the problem?

The announcer being ever so tactful, was trying not to scare the judge. "Well I don't want to alarm you, but you have a visitor. You need to get out of there."

Randy was up and moving instantly, making his way across the ring. He spoke to the announcer as he went. "I am going straight across the ring, as fast as I can, and I'm not looking back."

When he did look back, he saw a large alligator slithering along the bank where he had just been seated. Apparently Randy hadn't been the only one to find the sunny spot appealing.

Maybe Canadian winters aren't so bad, after all.

⤙ Josi

The mare was wired. Sitting on her, Sharon had the unsettling feeling that she was perched on a keg of dynamite with a disturbingly short fuse.

They were at the Harwinton Fair Horse Show where the mare was entered in several classes. But there was no way Sharon was about to go in them, not with the way this mare felt!

Of course, the mare was new. Seven year old Southern Missouri State University Josi Bar had just arrived at their home Thursday night. Today was Sunday. Neither Sharon nor Todd Cipolla had had a chance to ride her since her arrival.

The show was one of their favorites. With a laid back attitude, good judges and good competition, they tried never to miss it. It was guaranteed to be a good time. Besides, the day was glorious: the vibrant colors around them a perfect example of a New England fall day.

Josi had been purchased as a broodmare. Sharon bought her based on her conformation and bloodlines. A Quarter Horse breeder, Sharon couldn't resist Josi's lineage: a granddaughter of Three Bars on top and Blondy's Dude on the bottom. With breeding like that, it didn't matter to Sharon if she could be ridden or not.

Yet, she had been used in the college's lesson program in the horsemanship classes and was supposed to be a great riding horse. So, why not try her out?

Todd had been the first one on her back. She was awesome. Just tucked in her nose and floated at a trot, then a smooth transition into a lope. A subtle shift of your seat and rise of the rein and she would back right up. She side passed as well as any grand prix dressage horse. And boy could she spin! Watching, Sharon couldn't wait to get on herself!

When she did, she was blown away! The mare was wonderful. But, and it was a big "but," she *was* wired. Electric. Sharon couldn't trust her to go into the show ring like that. So she focused on working off some of that energy in the practice ring. She missed her classes, but the trail class was still to come. She asked Todd to take Josi in the trail class.

The trail class required Josi to cross bridges, open and close a gate, retrieve mail from a mailbox, and perform over rails on the ground. They started out just fine. But things quickly deteriorated. They came to the gate, which consisted of a piece of rope strung between posts about 12 feet apart. The rope was looped over one post. Todd opened it with no problem, removing the rope from the post it was fastened around. But putting it back was a whole different story. Todd's general plan of attack would be to ride through, spin on the haunches to face the gate, and then close it.

Josi walked through, and then did a nice spin to face the gate. But then she went into reverse, with no plan to change gears. As the rope got tighter and tighter, Todd leaned out of the saddle, trying desperately to hold on.

Soon his arm was outstretched as far as it could go, then his fingertips were barely hanging on, and then, with one more slow step backwards the rope slipped out of his grasp.

Sharon, watching with her friend Cindy, couldn't help laughing. She also couldn't help thinking about the next obstacle: the bridge. It was a beautiful bridge. Unlike the usual piece of plywood laid on the ground, this was the genuine article, about 10 feet long with wood railings and flower pots filled with yellow mums lining the sides.

The mare took one look at it and it was clear that the bridge was in trouble. "Are you nuts? You want me to go over *that?*" was written all over her face.

Todd was just as determined that she would go over the bridge as she was that she would not. They reached a compromise. Josi put her front feet on the bridge. Then she showed off her side passing ability by walking sideways along the bridge, wiping out the mums with her hind feet. In case she hadn't quite made her point, she then swung around to the other side of the bridge, taking out those mums as well.

Todd knew that the class was history, so he signaled to let the judges know that he was withdrawing from the competition. However, he would continue the course as a training experience for the mare.

The judges put their clipboards down. They had been trying to control their laughter; now they didn't have to. The audience was enjoying the spectacle and Todd couldn't help laughing as well.

Josi was supposed to trot over the ground poles that comprised the next obstacle. Somehow, through an adept show of athleticism, she managed to land on every one. The geometry of the exercise was completely rearranged.

The next goal was to do a turn on the forehand in the "box" which consisted of a square chalk line in the dirt. Using her hooves as the point of an eraser, she skidded around the line, erasing most of the chalk.

The poles she was supposed to weave through? They were swiftly dispatched in every direction.

While Josi was busy obliterating the rest of the trail course, the ring crew occupied themselves by rescuing the fallen mums. They replaced them neatly alongside the bridge.

Out of the corner of his eye, Todd could see the ring crew restoring the mum display. Apparently Josi saw them too.

Reaching the last obstacle, the mailbox, Josi halted perfectly alongside it. Todd should have known he was being set up. As he reached into it for his bag of candy, she went right back into her world class side pass—away from the box. Todd found himself in the now familiar position of desperately hanging on, stretching his arm out in an attempt to hold on to the bag of candy. He held on so well that soon the mailbox was leaning precariously in his direction. It was time to let go.

The mailbox sprang back to center, spooking Josi across the ring to the freshly rescued mums. The poor ring crew looked on in dismay as she scored a strike, wiping out the yellow flowers for the second time.

Todd wasn't about to end on that note. He pushed the mare back to the mailbox: leaving a bag of candy behind was *not* an option. Managing to retrieve it, he shot his fist in the air in a triumphant YES! The crowd cheered!

Todd patted the mare and rode out of the ring. So he didn't win the class. He had a good laugh and a great time. And after all, that's what he came for.

⟶ The Trail Ride

Imagine that you just moved to a new barn. You want to settle in, make friends, have someone to ride with, to show you the trails. Another boarder comes up to you. The boarder knows you're new and very kindly asks if you would like to accompany him on a trail ride.

What would you do?

Most of us would be like Richard. We would say "sure." Richard had only had his horse Vic, for about a year, and had been riding just a little longer than that. So he wasn't the world's most experienced rider. When he agreed to the trail ride, he had no idea what he was getting himself into.

So, off they went. The trail system was one of the most beautiful in the country, the paths sprawling through the campus and estates of Old Westbury, on Long Island.

Richard was riding Vic, a three-quarter Thoroughbred, one-quarter Percheron cross. David, the other boarder, was riding Sinbad, a towering Thoroughbred that made Vic look like a large pony.

Richard's first clue that this might not be an average trail ride was when he realized David was lacking a hard hat.

"You're not wearing a helmet" he commented.

"I don't need one," was the reply.

At this point Richard was still under the impression that he was riding with a normal person.

As they rode, the two carried on a conversation. Soon, David decided to pick up the pace. "How about a canter?" he asked.

"Sure," answered Richard.

They both picked up a canter and tried to continue talking. It was a bit difficult to hear each other at this pace, so Richard turned to face his fellow trail rider, hoping he would be able to better understand him.

What he saw so surprised him that he nearly fell off Vic. He tried to say something but no words could come forth. This was highly unusual for a lawyer who prided himself on his oratory skills. But so was the sight that beheld him.

David was not sitting in the saddle. He was standing on it. Backwards.

As Richard struggled to regain his balance, both in the saddle and in his composure, David cantered past, twirled stylishly around so that he faced forward, and ducked to avoid a low hanging branch.

"Let's jump," he yelled, apparently unaware of the effect that he had just had on Richard.

Dazed, Richard merely nodded.

Sinbad took off as though a starting gate had been slammed open, and the three quarters of Vic that came from Thoroughbred ancestry took full control. He was going to keep up with that horse (if not catch him) and that was that. There would be no argument.

Somewhere in Richard's memory words like "control" and "balance" were lurking. He knew that this fanatical gallop was not how one was supposed to approach a fence. But he had no say in the matter.

These fences were not small potatoes. They were big, solid, cross country fences: panels and stone walls and coops. Fences that many experienced riders would have thought twice before jumping, and poor Richard, with barely a year's experience, was jumping them at warp speed. Vic, he noticed, was enjoying himself immensely. Richard, on the other hand, was wondering who on earth he had decided to go trail riding with.

Finally they slowed. They resumed talking and Richard gave no hint about his surprise concerning the nature of this trail ride. Things seemed almost normal when Richard glanced to his right, where Sinbad was. He saw feet in midair. David was standing on his hands on the saddle, his body straight up, upside down.

Both Vic and Richard did manage to return to the barn physically unscathed.

Word spreads quickly at any barn, and soon other boarders were coming up to Richard.

"Are you *nuts?!!* Why on earth did you go out on a trail ride with David? I can't *believe* you did that!"

David, it turned out, was David Copeland, a stunt rider, and Sinbad was his stunt horse. One of David's accomplishments was serving as Arnold Schwarzenegger's stuntman for the movie "True Lies," In this movie David rode a horse into an elevator, onto (and almost off of) a roof, and galloped around Central Park jumping whatever he could find.

Everyone thought that he was crazy and couldn't believe the new boarder had gone out on trail with him.

Richard's answer was completely honest. "I just didn't know."

But when he was asked if he would do it again, he smiled. "Sure," he said.

⟿ Fire Horse

In the 19th century, and early into the 20th, horses moved America. They farmed our fields, transported people and goods, delivered mail and milk, and pulled the machinery that put out fires.

Fire horses had to be very special animals. Besides the speed, strength, and stamina needed to pull the heavy equipment, they also had to be intelligent and tractable.

In his younger days, the big black horse had been a fire horse. Entrusted with the lives of the citizens of Torrington, Connecticut, he had a crucial role to play in the workings of the city. He loved his job. When the alarm sounded, he would dance with excitement, anticipating the rush of flying out of the firehouse and tearing through the city streets.

But as he aged, he lost the critical speed necessary to be a fire horse. He found a second career, a life on the road crew of the town. Horses on the road crew pulled road graders, hauled equipment around in wagons, and did all the heavy work that trucks do today.

No one was quite sure of the breeding of the big horse, but there was definitely Percheron in his heritage. He was a good citizen, working hard, pulling heavy loads, standing stolidly while the crews worked to maintain the roads.

Then one day, the crew was working on South Main Street. The black gelding was, as always, doing his part, pulling his weight with the crew.

Suddenly, a bell was ringing. It was the fire alarm summoning firemen to their horses and a fire.

Like a flash, the black horse was gone, wagon swinging wildly behind him. No one could catch him, no one would dare try.

But he was easy to find. He was back at the firehouse, reporting for duty.

You Know You're Horse Crazy When You. . .

Cluck to your truck to help it get up a hill.

Know more about your horse's nutrition than your own.

Find mucking stalls a better mood lifter than Zoloft or Wellbutrin.

Engage in a hobby that is more work than your day job.

Paid more for your horse than you did for your home..

Believe that a fully loaded pickup truck is the ultimate driving machine.

Fail to associate whips, leather pants and chains with sexual deviancy.

Will end a relationship because of your horse.

Think nothing of eating a sandwich after mucking stalls.

Know why a thermometer has a strand of yarn attached to one end of it.

AND MORE....

⟶ Dressage4Kids

It started out as just a horse show. Not just any horse show to be sure, but a horse show. The idea was to get back to the basics.

Lendon Gray works with kids: lots of kids, many of them top notch riders.

But what she was seeing disturbed her. The kids had fancy horses. They could ride their own particular horse; they could execute a particular test. But they were lacking in basics, in horsemanship skills.

Lendon comes from a strong Pony Club background. In Pony Club you learned to be a horseperson, not just a rider. You learned the care of the horse: what to do with a case of thrush, proper feeding, how to clean a stall. Riding was part of it, certainly not all of it.

Lendon wanted her students (and other riders) to have the same skills, to broaden their knowledge, and she came up with an idea. She would have a show that was not just based on dressage tests. Instead, there would be three components: a dressage test, a dressage equitation class where riders would be judged as a group on position and basics, and a written test.

The written test would be based on assigned reading, and would cover both riding theory and stable management. It would also contain questions based on the prize list—because so many kids don't know the rules!

All three phases of the show would count equally, so the winner would not be determined by who had the fanciest horse. Lendon wanted to level the playing field and create a competition that would help develop the riders.

Divisions of dressage4kids (the "show" part is now called The Youth Dressage Festival and it takes place at the HITS facility in Saugerties, New York each August) range from Introductory Level all the way through Fourth, FEI Pony, Junior, Young Rider and Paraequestrian. Teams may be formed (made up in whatever fashion competitors wish) and they compete for the USDF Region 8 Championship.

One of the unique features of dressage4kids is the roving trainers at the show. Featuring such luminaries as Tom Noone and Courtney King, these trainers roam the show grounds helping kids who have signed up to ask for their assistance. Many of these kids attend the show without a trainer. Thanks to the roving trainers, the kids might have more schooling here in half an hour than they have had in the past year!

There are also roving judges who give awards to whatever catches their eye and pleases them. The award might be to the "pony with the fluffiest tail," the best "little brother groom" or the best "smile at the end of a test." These awards can make the day for a child who is having a tough week or bring joy to a child who has never won an award before in his life.

The atmosphere at dressage4kids is not like your typical dressage show. Rather than stress in the air, there is a sense of fun, of anticipation.

Kids on tiny ponies of unknown origin mingle with riders on Dutch warmblood stallions—and everything in between!

Many farms show up in "team uniforms" so they can be easily spotted. Competitors clad in pink polo shirts, for example might all hail from Frazier Farms in Woodbury, Connecticut.

The roving trainers at dressage4kids aren't the only illustrious names on the grounds. The judges are the best of the best and have included Robert Dover, Carol Lavelle and Michael Poulin.

On the Saturday evening of the show, a dinner is held. Here the judges have a chance to speak about what they saw that day, or to give advice to the kids. Some judges, says Lendon, have been "awe inspiring." Carol Lavell gave a great talk about the necessity of learning how to compete in the extreme heat. Many if not most Olympics and World Games have been held during the heat of summer.

Kids at the show have to volunteer one hour of their time to the show. There are plenty of jobs to choose from; they can be runners, tote water, or whatever else needs to be done. It's a great way for them to get a sense of what goes into putting a show together.

It's also a great way to get acquainted with riders from other countries. Foreign teams, invited by Lendon, also compete. Although superstars such as Germany have come in the past, Lendon makes an effort to invite some countries that are not necessarily in the forefront of dressage, such as South Africa or Brazil.

And—surprise! It's not just dressage riders who win—both eventers and hunter riders have won classes at the show, and once it was a hunter rider who took home the overall title.

Twice the overall high score rider has been a foreigner. These riders have to do everything the same as their American counterparts. They don't, however, have to import their horses, as Lendon finds mounts for them, horses that are generously donated for the occasion.

The show proved successful. so successful in fact, that it took on a life of its own. Volunteers appeared, "amazingly generous people" who helped the show grow and become more and more as time went on.

Lendon views dressage4kids as an opportunity to educate anyone interested in dressage, and runs it in an effort to help develop young riders. She makes sure that, not only is it educational, but it's fun, too!

Dressage4kids remains a separate entity, not part of something else, quite intentionally. Lendon wanted to keep it that way to insure that it was about the kids, to make them "front and center."

As well as awarding both team and individual trophies, the festival is known for its abundance of Hi Score Awards, such as Hi Score Morgan, Arab, and Thoroughbred. It also has a Prix Caprilli (which is a dressage test with jumps) and a Musical Freestyle, both of which are separate classes. The show recently added what is surely the first ever dressage trail class!

Kids participating in the Youth Dressage Festival are also taught to jog. In international competitions (CDI) riders have to jog their horses for soundness. Riders are taught how to dress and how to turn their horses out. This prepares those who are looking to progress so when they get there, they know what to expect and are not caught by surprise.

As the show grew and became profitable, the question was raised—what to do with the profits?

The answer was easy. The profits turned into a scholarship fund for kids to further their riding education. Any kid was eligible to apply as long as they competed in the show. It didn't matter if they won or if they placed last, the only requirement was that they competed, or took part in some other activity.

The scholarships are for education use only and usually are for about $500-$600, although they can run to as much as two thousand for a kid going to Europe.

Written reports must be prepared after the training is completed, detailing just what the experience was like.

As the show grew, as interest grew, it developed a life of its own. No longer was it just a show, it was now a not for profit organization.

Lendon, wanting to do still more, asked the kids what they would like. Out of this came the Weekend Education Program, which is comprised of two days of lectures and talks by various experts. The program, held in the winter, changes every year and includes a variety of subjects. Due to popular demand, it is now open to adults as well.

Soon, the Tuesday afternoon clinic was born. Lendon wanted to bring dressage to everyone—hunter riders, eventers, anybody with an interest.

The clinic consists of a demonstration/lecture, study sessions and a lesson. They are all taught by Lendon and her staff members. The clinic begins as a group and then splits into private sessions.

Next came the FEI pony clinic, taught by Cornelia Endres, chef d'equpe of the (undefeated) German pony team. This was a natural for Lendon, who is known for taking the pony Seldom Seen to the top ranks of the dressage world, and a real champion of the pony in the dressage ring.

In its first year the pony clinic barely had enough participants, and they were an eclectic group. It has now grown to the point where it is a three day clinic consisting of all top ponies competing at the FEI level.

The pony clinic led to the first ever all pony dressage show (for adults and kids) which took place as part of the CDI at Saugerties, New York, in August.

The whole phenomenon of dressage4kids has grown into a huge tree of many branches out of the back to basics seed. Lendon's amazing volunteer committee has been in large part responsible for it. "Some have kids, some don't have kids, some of them don't even ride!" They are, says Lendon, "just the greatest group of people!"

The committee meets once a month, and Lendon is thrilled to note that kids who once rode in dressage4kids have now graduated and are on the committee.

The kids Lendon helped educate, following in her footsteps, now educate other kids. In dressage4kids, Lendon has created an entity that has far outgrown its original scope. The program flourishes as it takes on greater dimensions and new directions. It touches the lives of increasing numbers of kids, as well as adults and yet never strays from its basic premise: the basics!

For more information, you can consult the website:
www.dressage4kids.com.

⟿ Missy

She's not your typical horse lover. Her eyes are round, and golden, with green glints. Her legs and feet are white, but not, like the rest of us, because we spend our daylight hours encased in breeches or jeans and boots.

She can jump as high as any horse, but then again she doesn't have to carry a rider.

Missy is a horse lover in feline form. Some cats are "people" cats: Missy is a "horse cat." Wherever the two horses of the farm in Kent, Connecticut, where Missy lives are found, Missy will be found as well. If they're in the barn, Missy is either curled up in the shavings of the stalls or snuggled into the hay bales piled alongside the stall walls. If they're out in the pasture, so is Missy. Like the postman of legend, neither rain, snow, heat nor extreme cold keeps her from her rounds with her equine partners.

People who come to the barn often ask "what's out there with the horses?" They are always surprised that a cat would lie curled up in a field between two grazing horses.

Tucker and HT are well aware that Missy is their cat. Sometimes she chooses to take a nap right in the middle of a flake of their hay. The horses will look the flake over carefully, and then gently, ever so gently, pull strands of hay out of the corners so as not to disturb their sleeping friend.

There are other cats on the farm. Missy doesn't particularly care. She ignores them. The horses are her friends.

One day, HT colicked. Badly. He would crash to his knees and thrash violently before being roused back to his feet. Missy perched on the Dutch door, watching with concern over her sick buddy, fretting until the vet came.

Once HT responded nicely to some oil and a shot of Banamine, he stood quietly in the stall with his head down. Missy walked over to him and stood on her hind legs in the shavings, rubbing her head against his nose. "I'm glad you're all right now, buddy," she clearly conveyed.

Horse lovers come in all forms.

⟶ Norm and Vinnie

J ohn Blair was not impressed. The videotape was of two draft horses pulling a wagon. They were big, grey, clunky looking horses, half Percheron, with manes down to their shoulders.

And what was he supposed to do with these horses? Well, the woman with the tape wanted him to teach her cart horses to jump.

The two horses, she said, were "Spanish Normans," and they ressembled the horses knights of the middle ages rode for jousting, and more importantly, for battle. The horses were a cross between a Percheron and an Andalusian.

They came with foreign sounding names that were difficult to pronounce, so John simplified things. They became Norm and Vinnie. Vinnie lived up to (or down to) John's first impressions. He couldn't jump worth a lick, splintering rails that were only 12 inches high. John attempted to give a lesson on Vinnie to Abby, the owner's daughter, and it proved disastrous. She had halted him and when she attempted to nudge him forward, instead of forward, he went down. Apparently Vinnie just forgot to move his legs.

Norm was another story. Norm was crazy. Big and crazy, not a good combination. Norm lived with his halter on because that was the only way you could catch him. And when John started to ride him, Norm did not want to trot or canter. Like the horses he was bred after, he wanted to . . .*charge*!

John spent a lot of time working with Norm. It was worth it, because, despite John's trepidations, Norm could jump. He jumped so high and so hard John was afraid the horse was going to smack his chin with his knees. And he was brave. You had to be careful where you aimed him because if it was in front of him, Norm was going over it. Banks, ditches, tables, nothing stopped him.

In time John felt that Norm was ready for a show. But he had to think about how he was going to handle it. The idea of appearing on the showgrounds with this horse embarrassed him. He had thought initially that it was ludicrous to try to teach this clunky carthorse to jump, and he knew that people looking at him would think the same thing. Maybe a name change would help the situation, dress him up a bit. So Norm became Sir Norman of Tiverton.

The initial reaction to Norm was, predictably, part skepticism and part ridicule. No one believed the cart horse could jump. But John hadn't believed it either.

Ridicule rapidly changed to admiration. And the admiration spread. Soon Norm developed his own fan club. Maybe he moved like an eggbeater and looked like he should be pulling a plow, but this horse could jump! And when he jumped, people came to watch. No one could miss Norm. His tremendous size and unique movement were unmistakable. The earth is shaking, buildings are swaying, and you're not in California? Norm must be in the ring.

The first year John had Norm, the horse earned the title "Spanish/Norman of the Year."

His fan club continues to grow, and he continues to draw people to the ring. He's not built to jump, he's not bred to jump, but jump he does—from the heart.

Professionals go by now, those same professionals that laughed when John showed up with the big grey plowhorse, and they say "How's Norm today?"

Although Norm will never be gorgeous, he has, with work, become a good looking horse. What was before pure mass has now become defined muscle. Norm is a powerhouse. And the crazy horse that arrived that day at John's barn has become a sweetheart, the kind of horse that all trainers dream of for their amateur riders. If Norm's rider, Gretchen, misses a distance, Norm just covers up and keeps on going. "Come on" he says to Gretchen, "Just hang in there and we can do it." They win all the time. Norm never stops, he's never lame, and he'll do *anything* for you if you scratch his ears.

And Vinnie? Whatever became of Vinnie? Well, he was donated to the police department. Only problem was, he flunked the test. He was not suited for the police or for life in the big city. So Vinnie came back to live next door to John and his wife Chris. He spends most of his time splintering fences and looking for trouble in the neighborhood.

As Chris put it, regarding Vinnie and Norm, "One's a bum, and one's a star."

⌁ STONEWALL JACKSON

There are a lot of ways to make a point, and nobody could accuse Al of a lack of imagination.

Al was a horseman skilled in the art of multi-tasking, whether he was training horses for the track, or training show horses, or teaching riders at the barn behind his house in Colts Neck, New Jersey.

Stonewall Jackson was one of his racehorses, a very handsome grey gelding. Stonewall retired from the track at the age of five, Well, maybe retired wouldn't be the best choice of words. Thrown off would be a bit closer to the truth.

Stonewall would train well enough. It was only when it came to race day that his issues came to light. Stonewall would step onto the track, a striking horse looking for all the world like a star. Then the announcer would speak and it was all over. Stonewall turned into a star all right, a rodeo star. Wrong venue, however, so off the track he went.

Luckily, failed racehorses always had other career options with Al. Al decided Stonewall could now be a show horse. He was beautiful, a good mover and with a little schooling he soon proved he could jump as well. His future was looking so bright he might need shades.

Alas, the reality of Stonewall's show career soon proved less than stellar.

Stonewall would go around beautifully—for a while. Then someone would spoil it all by picking up a microphone. Stonewall became a bucking dervish, dumped his rider, and ran madly about the show grounds until someone could catch him.

Stonewall's show career, like his race career, ended ignominiously. That was all right, though. He still had another option: he could teach kids to ride. He did this job well, turning into a fine school horse and earning his keep.

Al was disappointed that Stonewall hadn't lived up to his potential. But it didn't take long to find him the perfect job.

Sometimes when kids do well they get too big for their britches. They get cocky, too sure of themselves. It doesn't make for pleasant company and it irritated Al like mad. All it took was for a kid to do well in a show or two and suddenly they thought they were Olympic material.

There was a cure for this, though, and the cure involved Stonewall. Say a kid had just been champion last week at a show and was really crowing about it. Al would mention casually that another show was coming up next week. Stonewall would be available. The kid would light up. Of course they wanted to ride the classy grey horse at the next show. Wouldn't everyone notice!

On the morning of the show Stonewall would look beautiful. Sparkly clean and ready to win. All would be well until the first time that loudspeaker went off. The results were always the same. Stonewall was loose, running around the show grounds, and the kid was in the dirt. Unhurt, but with an ego shaken down to size.

They were right, too, everyone noticed!

Stonewall may have been a failure at his first two careers, but in his third he finally found his niche and proved himself a star!

⤳ Gillette

He was a mistake, but a happy mistake.

His dam, a Percheron mare named Ruby, belonged to Kate Keeney when she owned a horse and carriage service in York, Pennsylvania. Kate moved to Connecticut to pair up with another carriage business and brought Ruby with her. During the moving process Ruby lived for a while at a friend's farm, a Percheron breeder.

Once Ruby arrived, she was put to work at Mystic Seaport, doing carriage rides. She was a Houdini, often escaping from her stall. In fact she was so good at escaping that she could both open a latch and unsnap a snap to earn her freedom. One night Kate got a call from the Mystic Police, wondering if the big white horse running through downtown Mystic had perhaps come from the museum. She had.

After that, the workers at the Seaport added a rope across her door to keep her enclosed.

Despite her penchant for exploring the area on her own, she was a good carriage horse, and earned her keep. The following summer, employees at the Seaport began to remark about how chubby Ruby had become. Then her farrier noticed Ruby's udder and the secret was revealed. "She's about to foal!" he said. Two days later, Gillette was born.

Gillette took after his mom with his mischievous nature and his beautiful good looks. After several years working at the seaport, he was purchased by Elaine Keeley, who had often driven Ruby while working there. He moved to Cedar Knoll Farm in Lisbon, Connecticut, owned by Elaine and her partner Terry Joseph, where he soon became one of their most popular carriage horses.

He also demonstrated just how like his mother he was. The farm has both standing and box stalls. Gillette lives in the end standing stall, near the hay drop and the side doors. One cold morning Elaine came to the barn for morning chores. She was looking at all the draft behinds lined up neat as a pin but when she counted there was a problem. One seemed to be missing. Gillete had slipped his halter and relocated himself to the hay drop, where he was contentedly munching on loose hay. Although there are now butt chains across the back of the stalls to keep the horses contained, Gillette still manages to lose his halter regularly, no matter how tightly it is strapped on.

Elaine is the first to admit that the star of her operation is "Very conceited. He's beautiful and he knows it, with his pure white coat, intelligent face and alert eye." His mane and tail are long and silky, his tail in addition thick and wavy. When Gillette is all cleaned up for a wedding, he glows.

Elaine, in addition to running the livery business, is an extremely accomplished artist who chooses draft horses as her primary works of art. And Gillette, with his stunning beauty, is one of her favorite subjects. It is also his portrait that serves as the logo for the farm's gift shop.

At 17 hands, with a weight of about 1800 pounds, Gillette is sure to attract attention. He is proud of his job and does it well. He stands quietly in harness no matter what kinds of noises and distractions are going on. He stands so quietly, in fact, that people sometimes wonder if he's real! People just itch to stroke his handsome face. But don't. Gillette will turn his head away and make a peculiar face. "Don't touch me," he communicates quite clearly.

Gillette in particular, and all of Cedar Knoll's horses have appeared in many newspapers and tourist brochures. Wherever they go, they get noticed.

Weddings are a staple of Gillette's career. For these he is often paired with Cedar Knoll's black vis-à-vis. Black carriages were used by royalty for formal affairs such as coronations and weddings. Elaine finds that the black vis-à-vis with its plush burgundy seats makes an elegant contrast to the bride.

There is one wedding that Elaine will never forget. They had shipped Gillette and the carriage over to Greenport, Long Island (New York) on the Orient Point Ferry. The girl who had hired them was the daughter of a very prominent businessman in town.

After driving to her house they picked her up, along with her father, and took them to the church for the ceremony. When the ceremony was over, they drove back to town: down Main Street to the docks for more pictures.

It soon became very clear to Elaine and Terry why they had been hired to drive Gillette for this wedding. On that day, there were three weddings in Greenport. One bride hired a typical limousine. Another chose an antique car. But there was no mistaking who got the most attention. As they pranced down Main Street, people poured out of stores and restaurants onto the sidewalks, cheering and waving and yelling their congratulations to the bride and groom in the horse drawn carriage.

When the local paper came out, the newlyweds in the wedding carriage were on the front cover.

All brides want their wedding day to be special. All the time, effort and planning go into making it that one perfect day: a day when they are the center of everyone's attention. Thanks to Gillette and the beautiful carriage no one will forget that wedding. There was no contest: the beautiful horse pulling the historic carriage was the only wedding in town that day.

GLOSSARY

automatic changes: When jumping a course of fences, a horse or pony has to remain on the correct lead. If they land from a fence on the wrong lead, they need to do a flying change to the correct one. Horses who do this on their own, or with the lightest of aids, are considered to have automatic changes

black type: in a racetrack program, a horse who is listed in "black type" is a stakes winner. Stakes races are the highest echelon in horse racing

dam: a horse's mother

flatting: a term hunter/jumper riders use to mean they are not jumping, only working at the walk, trot and canter

14.3 hands: This is the worst height you would want for a horse in hunter competition. It's a nightmare for pony breeders, who hope that their stock never gets over 14.2 hands, which makes them ineligible for pony classes. They would then have to compete against horses, when they often don't have enough stride for the longer distances, or are not big enough to jump the bigger fences

hand: the unit of measurement for a horse, it equals four inches

hunter: Hunters are judged on the flat on how well they move, their manners, their condition and their turn-out. Over fences they are again judged on movement and manners, in addition how well they jump the fences, how consistent they are. Hunters are subjectively judged, like figure skaters

in and out: two jumps in a line with either one or two strides between them

jumper: Jumpers are judged objectively—they have to jump fast and they have to leave the fences up, but other than that it doesn't matter how they do it

Levels of Jumper Classes: Jumper classes range from Level 0 to Level 9. Level 0 is 2'9" in height, Level 1 is 3'0" in height, with spreads from 3'0"-3'6". Each level after that is 3" higher and 3" wider

line: a line is two or more fences in a row, sometimes it is a straight line, sometimes it can be a bending line

liverpool: a water jump

"off the eye": Individual fences are ridden "off the eye," in other words there is no set number of strides leading to the fence, so the rider (in some cases the horse!) needs to choose the distance. In a line of fences, the distances are set so that they equal a certain number of strides, so you might hear a trainer say, "That's a five stride line."

oxer: a wide fence, with two sections. Usually, the front section is lower, with a higher rear section, but sometimes both sections can be the same height, This is called a square oxer

sire: a horse's father

spread: a wide fence, it can be an oxer, a triple bar, or a water jump

sprinter: a racehorse who can run very fast, but not for long distances, is termed a "sprinter."

stayer: a racehorse with more stamina, who can win at the longer distances *swapping:* changing leads (flying changes)

vertical: a jump in which all the elements are in the same plane, not a spread fence like an oxer.

We will be doing a Volume III. If you have a story you would like to share, let us know! Stories may be about any breed or discipline, but they must be upbeat stories—funny, inspirational or informational. You can contact Ann at: loveofthehorse@sbcglobal.net. Thanks!

ANN JAMIESON

Ann Jamieson is a United States Equestrian Federation judge licensed in hunters, jumpers and hunt seat equitation. She shows her own horse, Fred Astaire, in hunters and First Level dressage.

Ann has written numerous articles for magazines and newspapers. She currently writes for "Today's Equestrian" magazine.

This is Ann's second volume of "For the Love of the Horse." A third volume is in the works, as well as a fiction novel (set in the horse show world).

Ann lives in Kent, Connecticut with her Occicat Hobbes.